Jump Start Your Career
in Technology & IT
in about 100 Pages

Table of Contents

Let's Start !

Introduction

In this day and age of distributed applications, database systems are two a penny. These data storage servers are cloud-based and server-based; even individual mobile phones have their own small-scale database systems.

Since everything needs some kind of data store to provide mass storage of any data generated by or attached to the application in question, the market is simply a minefield.

This e-book is about a database system that for the most part has quietly remained in the shadows while other systems, such as those developed by Oracle, Microsoft and many others, have hogged the limelight. The database in question, however, has in fact been around for a considerably long time, in some cases before many of the more popular ones.

This database is known as Postgres, and it is one of the longest running, most stable open source database systems available on the market today.

Let's take a tour of this remarkable data storage server and its many facilities.

Chapter 1 What is Postgres?

In simple terms, PostgreSQL, known as Postgres, is just another database management system, no different from the ones you may already be familiar with using, such as Microsoft SQL Server, MySQL, or even MongoDB.

In more descriptive terms, Postgres is much more than any of those others that I've just mentioned. It's not just a regular run-of-the-mill DBMS, but a fully-fledged data management solution that runs on many different platforms.

Postgres has been around way longer than many of the database systems we know and love today. Over the years it has evolved from a simple data management solution in a university to a data management solution that many people agree rivals things like Oracle 10/11/12g and other heavyweights.

It also has additional products that support large scale clustering, spatial and GIS services, communications industry-specific functionality, financial industry-specific functionality, distributed processing, and much more.

It's a DBMS that has stood the test of time, and proven that it has both the backing and the power to take on any data management task you can think of. And the best part about it all?

It's FREE. It's an open source project that's free to use, free to download and free to modify. In fact, there are a large number of variants out there from commercial to free that are based largely on Postgres, parts of the core Postgres engine and parser, or both. So not only is it a great all-around DBMS, but it's also an infinitely expandable data management toolkit.

Chapter 2 Why Postgres

Given that this book is being published by a .NET tools company, and I am predominantly a .NET developer (even if I do work across various platforms), the million dollar question has to be asked: Why use Postgres when we have MS SQL Server, MongoDB, and many .NET-specific database systems at our disposal?

Well, let's get the obvious one out of the way, which I've already mentioned: it's free. More than that though, it's open. The Postgres open source license allows you to pretty much do anything you want with the application and its code. This includes customizing it for your own in-house purposes and specific needs.

If customizing the core application is not for you, then its highly flexible extension API can be used to create add-on products that integrate into the core system as though they were an integral part that had always been there.

What else can it do?

Postgres over the years has developed some very unique features that simply don't exist in other databases. I'll list some of these soon. It's also fully 100% compliant with ANSI SQL:2008 standards and runs on many different platforms, including Windows and all flavors of Linux, Unix, and even the likes of Solaris and all recent editions of MacOS. It's also easy to install on all these platforms; in most cases, it's as simple as installing a single package.

Postgres is also very scalable and has some very impressive upper limits on what it can and cannot achieve.

Table 1: *Postgres Limits*

Limit Type	Limit Value
Maximum Database Size	Unlimited
Maximum Table Size	32 Terabytes
Maximum Row Size	1.6 Terabytes
Maximum Field/Column Size	1 Gigabyte
Maximum Rows per Table	Unlimited

Limit Type	Limit Value
Maximum Columns per Table	250 to 1600 depending on column types
Maximum Indexes per Table	Unlimited

As you can see, these are some very impressive statistics. The reason so much is unlimited is because Postgres stores its databases in regular files in the host file system, so the only realistic upper limit is available disk space.

Postgres also has many different types of indexes available to ensure efficient data access. I'll cover these in more detail in later chapters, but for now the following indexes are available out of the box:

- B-Tree
- Hash
- GiST
- GIN

New index strategies can easily be added using the extension API, just as easily as new data types, table types, storage types and many other things.

Moving on, Postgres is also a fully object-oriented database, meaning it's designed to model data in the same way as object-oriented programming languages like C++ and C#.

Some of the features in the core product are available specifically to support this scenario, the most useful of which is table inheritance.

Table Inheritance

Table inheritance is the process of using database tables in a similar manner to how a developer might extend the functionality in an object-oriented application architecture, allowing the reuse of existing data items, while adding new data items to the table.

Let me give you an example.

Let's assume we have the following database table for our company staff:

FullName	Full name of the staff member
WageBand	The wage band this staff member is in

PhoneNumber	Office phone number of this person
Department	Which department this staff member works in

It's a fairly simple, standard table definition typical of something that might be found in a normal database.

Let's now assume that each department has its own specific attributes it wishes to keep for each staff member in that department, and let's further assume that each department has different requirements for these attributes.

So for example, the IT department may have the following additions:

- Languages developed in
- Courses taken
- Projects worked on
- Systems owned

The Accounts department might have the following:

- Clients responsible for
- Projects worked on
- Subdepartment
- Office name

In most database systems, you would have to extend your database table to ensure it had all the required fields needed for each of those departments:

FullName	Full name of the staff member
WageBand	What wage band this staff member is in
PhoneNumber	Office phone number of this person
Department	Which department this staff member works in
Languages	Languages this staff member can develop with
CoursesTaken	Courses this staff member has taken

Projects	Projects this staff member has been involved in
Systems	Systems this staff member is responsible for
Clients	Clients this staff member is responsible for
SubDepartment	Which subdepartment this staff member is part of
OfficeName	Which district office this staff member works from

Developers have had to deal with this scenario for a long time now, so why does it matter? Well, it's simple to define this when you first create your database, but what about adding a new department to your system several years after the database was originally created?

Postgres solves this issue with its table inheritance capability. Essentially, it allows you to define the original staff table, as normal. It then allows you to define additional tables with just the extra columns, which "inherits" from the original staff table.

The result is two tables that look like the following:

FullName	Full name of the staff member
WageBand	What wage band this staff member is in
PhoneNumber	Office phone number of this person
Department	Which department this staff member works in
Languages	Languages this staff member can develop with
CoursesTaken	Courses this staff member has taken
Projects	Projects this staff member has been involved in
Systems	Systems this staff member is responsible for

and

FullName	Full name of the staff member
WageBand	What wage band this staff member is in
PhoneNumber	Office phone number of this person
Department	Which department this staff member works in
Projects	Projects this staff member has been involved in
Clients	Clients this staff member is responsible for looking after
SubDepartment	Which subdepartment this staff member is part of
OfficeName	Which district office this staff member works from

The table inheritance capability does much more than just save typing time.

If you change the **FullName, WageBand, PhoneNumber**, or **Department** fields of the previous staff table for example, those changes are made to the parent staff table and the IT staff table.

This way, you can have an application that filters its records based on the department the staff member works in, and shows only the data needed by that department. Someone in another department can still see the basic details of that person from their own application, should they need to.

Essentially, you're treating the table like a reusable object that can be extended infinitely. Even more so, inherited tables can be further inherited themselves in the same manner.

Imagine how useful this is in an environment where you're frequently adding new functionality to an application. Rather than create scripts to migrate existing tables to a new schema then possibly have to update many different ORM or data access mechanisms to see the new schema, you can simply add an inherited table to your database, and then add a new class to your data access layer to access only that new, extended table. Existing code will continue to work as normal, and your new functionality will continue as though it has that new table.

Yes, there is more...

Multiple languages embedded directly inside the database allow you to write stored procedures in the following languages (the first four are included out of the box):

- pgSQL / SQL
- Tcl
- Python
- Perl
- C
- C++
- R
- Java
- PHP
- Ruby
- Scheme

...and many others.

All of these procedural languages have normal first class syntax constructions too. Things like For-Each, Do-While, If-Then, and many other constructs work on full table sets directly inside a stored procedure in exactly the same manner as they do with normal applications in the real world.

This pretty much means that language skills you've already acquired can easily be used in developing solutions directly inside the core product.

Moving on, we also have the concept of array types in a regular database column.

Arrays? In a database?

Yes, all of the Postgres default data types can be used as an array type.

What's more, when you have an array type, all of the available programming APIs available allow you to interface your application to Postgres to support these operations natively without any extra work. For example, you can easily define the following in C#:

```
int[] myIntegers = new int[]{1,2,3,4,5};
```

You can save this array directly into an array field in your database by using normal data access calls and then later retrieve that data field. Your array will remain intact for you to use as you would normally.

Postgres can also validate your data at insert and update times to ensure that you only put data into your database that is valid. Validation already exists for things like email addresses, phone numbers, regular expressions, and more.

So far pretty much everything I've mentioned is included out of the box. We haven't even begun to scratch the surface of the additions that are possible with the many extensions available, many of which are actually included with the core server in the extra contributions folder that is installed with the product.

These extensions allow you to manipulate XML and XSLT directly in the database, add extra encryption functionality, and add new data types (such as ISBN numbers for books) along with appropriate validation rules and logic to ensure that your types contain what you expect.

There are even full-blown feature packs that transform Postgres into something entirely different. Packages like PostGIS (there's a full chapter on it later in the book) transform a PostgreSQL server into a full-fledged GIS data management system with the same spatial functionality of Oracle Spatial.

As if that's not enough, the different versions of Postgres available for different platforms will take advantage of special facilities available on those platforms. For example, there is an x64 (64-bit specific) build for the Windows platform that allows you to have larger upper limits than those previously mentioned. There are builds available that will run across massively parallel super-scalar CPU architectures, and there's even specialist builds that can use things like a GPU for heavy duty number crunching.

For a free system, there is little reason not to choose Postgres as the data store for your application, and as you'll see later, with the latest round of .NET data providers available, the server plays very nicely with things like Entity Framework 4.1 and newer.

One final point I'd like to make is aimed at those who are worried about free products not having support.

Apart from the obvious open source community support that is available, EnterpriseDB (one of the main companies that looks after and runs the various Postgres projects) offers many support packages designed for companies that want to pay for support contracts. They also offer some massive extended professional packages and extensions for companies that wish to pay for the system. These extra packages take things even further than those facilities described so far in this book.

If you want to read more, the full feature matrix page can be viewed at http://www.postgresql.org/about/featurematrix/.

Chapter 3 A Brief History of Postgres

As is the case with many open source projects, Postgres was originally developed in 1986 at the University of California at Berkley (UCB). Developed by Michael Stonebraker, a member of the computer science faculty, Postgres was designed as a follow-up to his previous database system, Ingres, which was acquired by Computer Associates.

Over the next eight years, Stonebraker and his students continued to innovate and extend Postgres with many features never seen before in a data management system. Later, a commercial version of Postgres was spun off and became the Illustra Database System, which was purchased by the Informix Corporation and integrated into its universal server product. In 2001, Informix was purchased by IBM for $1 billion.

In 1995, two of Stonebraker's students, Andrew Yu and Jolly Chen, wrote the SQL interpreter within the core Postgres project and renamed the system Postgres95.

In 1996, Postgres95 was released into the open source community on a global scale, leaving its academic roots behind and entering a brave new world. Over the next eight years, Postgres95 was extended worldwide by an army of volunteers. During this time, the core server was made more stable, many regression tests and extensions were created for it, and much, much more.

The result has been a database system that is world-renowned as one of the most stable and feature-rich data management systems available today.

Today, PostgreSQL is monitored by the PostgreSQL Global Development Group, managed primarily by EnterpriseDB. The code base takes regular contributions from CISCO, NTT Data, NOAA, Research in Motion, Google, Fujitsu, and many other large players in the IT marketplace.

Chapter 4 Installing Postgres

Now that you've been introduced to Postgres and what it's capable of, it's time to actually install and play with it. Since I'm writing this book on a Windows-based machine, the instructions and illustrations will reflect that.

I will make comments as I go along with regard to installing the system on other operating systems, but unfortunately there is simply not enough space in this book to describe the installation process in detail for every platform available.

Obtaining the software

You can download everything you need from http://www.postgresql.org/download/.

You will find links for the various platforms, and also features such as live CD distributions so you can try applications before you install them.

Note that all Linux and Unix distributions that use a package manager such as apt-get or Yum also have their own distribution-specific Postgres packages available in their own repository. When possible, you should aim to use these rather than the generic versions available from the download page.

Distro-specific versions are usually tailored for the specific platform they run on, and often will take advantage of extra functionality not available on other platforms.

From the download page there is also a link to **pgFoundry**. I highly recommend exploring this in great depth, as there is a wealth of software available, from simple extensions to full packages like PostGIS. All of it is presented in a simple-to-use, web-based browser that feels very much like an ordinary file system browser with extended information.

You can also get every version of the software ever produced, going all the way back to v7.0.3, as a pre-compiled binary, or v1.08 as a source tree. At the time of writing this book, the most up-to-date version is v9.2.4.

Installing the server

For my purposes, and since I've already got production copies of Postgres installed on the PC I'm working on, I'll be installing this into a virtual machine running Windows 7 under VMware desktop.

The steps I'll describe are identical for other editions too. While we are on the subject of operating systems, I personally have not tried to see if Postgres will install on Windows 8, nor have I come across any information related to it. My personal view is that it's likely to work, as Windows 8 still has a classic desktop and command line available. I cannot, however, confirm whether it will cause any problems; all of my installs including the one for this book are on Windows 7, 64-bit.

Once you download the installer executable, double-click on it, just as you would any other installer. Please note that for the demos here I am using the 32-bit installation of Postgres. While there's no difference between the 32-bit and 64-bit installers, just be aware as with any app available as 32-bit and 64-bit, default path names and other choices may be different.

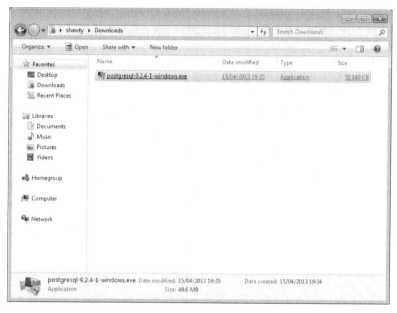

Figure 1: Postgres installer

First, you should see the normal **User Access Control** confirmation if you have it configured. Because Postgres is installed as a Windows service, it must be run with administrator permissions or the installation will not succeed.

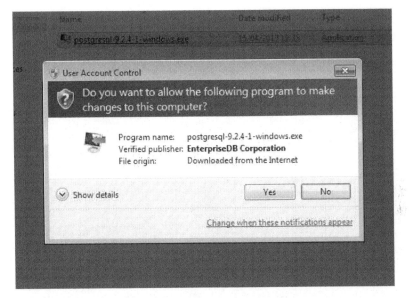

Figure 2: User Account Control window

Like with any normal application installer, click **Yes** to run an installation wizard that should be familiar to most Windows users.

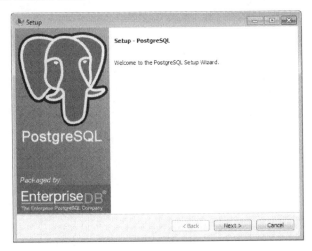

Figure 3: Postgres Setup wizard

Click **Next**, and you'll be asked for the location to install the server.

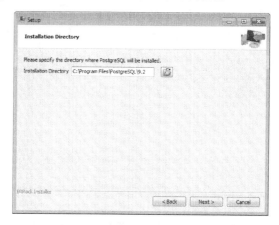

Figure 4: Installation Directory setup

You can click on the small folder button to graphically browse to a new location, or type one in the text box provided. Generally it's better to choose the defaults, as this will install it in the usual Program Files directory where other applications go.

The next page will ask for a path where you want Postgres to store its data files. These will be the physical files where Postgres stores the actual data, so you need to make sure these are located somewhere where there is enough disk space for your intended usage. It's wise to ensure these are stored in an entirely separate location from the application, but for the book's purposes I'll keep these two folders the same.

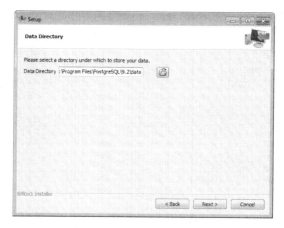

Figure 5: Data Directory setup

The next page you should see is the **Password** screen.

For readers familiar with SQL Server, the **postgres** account serves the same purpose as the **su** account. For readers more familiar with MySQL, this is the equivalent of the **Root** account.

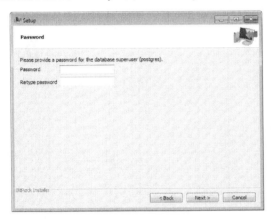

Figure 6: Password setup

You must keep this password safe since it allows access to all accounts on the server once it is up and running. It will be the only active account on the system until you add others.

Next you will be asked for the port number you wish the server to listen on. Unless you have special reasons for changing it, it's best to leave it as the default. The main reason this option exists is because Postgres allows you to run several different copies of the same server on the same machine, completely independent of each other and each other's data.

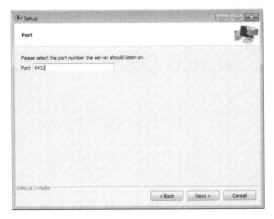

Figure 7: Port setup

The next page allows you to set a location-specific character set, or port number. It's best to leave this at the default location, which the installer will try to determine from your OS install language. Changing the port number is one of the biggest causes of failed Postgres installations. In such cases, the server is set up and running, populated with data, and then fails as soon as a script in a different location tries to access that data from a web server. Using the default port prevents this scenario from arising.

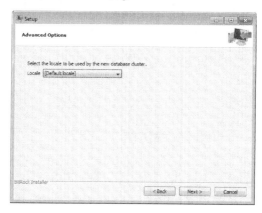

Figure 8: Advanced Options setup

The next page should be the confirmation that Postgres is ready to be installed. Click **Next** and wait a few minutes while things are set up.

If everything has gone according to plan, the final dialog box you see will ask if you want to run Stack Builder and invite you to click **Finish** to complete the installation. Ensure that the box to run Stack Builder is selected, and then click **Finish**.

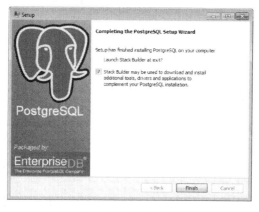

Figure 9: Completing the Setup Wizard

What is Stack Builder?

Stack Builder is a Windows-only component that allows you to install some of the many add-ons available for Postgres quickly and easily. You can use it to install access libraries for your programming projects, and complete toolkits to help manage your server.

Once you click **Finish** in the main installer you will be see the following:

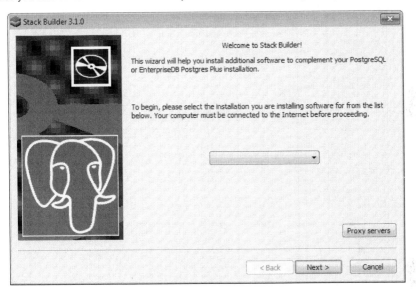

Figure 10: Stack Builder wizard

The first thing you need to do is select the Postgres server you've just installed using the drop-down menu in the middle of the page.

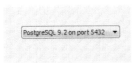

Figure 11: Server drop-down menu

If you need to, you can also use the **Proxy servers** button to set up any external access proxy information you may need. Since Stack Builder needs to access outside servers to download the software you choose, you may need to specify some options in there.

We don't need any proxy information, so once we select our running server, click **Next** to continue.

Stack Builder will access the **pgFoundry** servers and download an application list, which it will then present on screen, allowing you to choose the software you wish to install. I encourage you to become familiar with all the items available on this list.

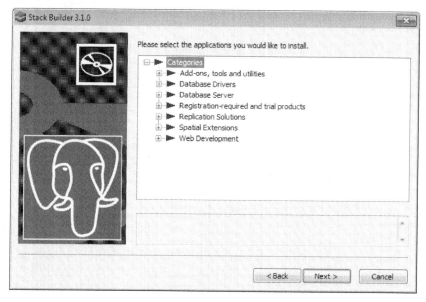

Figure 12: Stack Builder applications list

Since we'll be taking a look at PostGIS later in the book, and since we'll also be writing some sample .NET code to access the server, we'll select the PostGIS spatial extensions and the open source **Npgsql** .NET ADO interface library (which, for those using Visual Studio, is also available on NuGet).

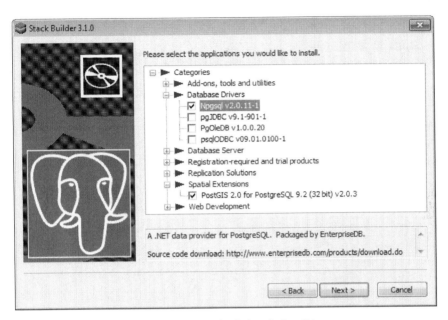

Figure 13: Stack Builder detailed applications list

Once you've finished selecting the additional products you want to install, click **Next** to continue.

The next page will ask you where you want to download the installers. Since these will be automatically run, you can just accept the defaults.

You will likely want to make a note of the location however, in case you want to back up the installers or run them again later on.

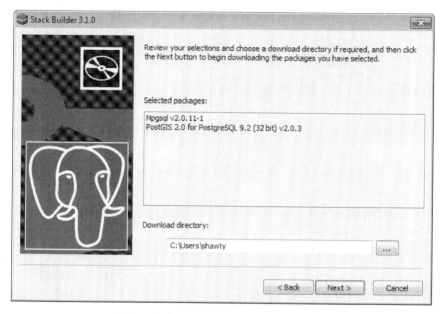

Figure 14: Stack Builder download directory

Click **Next** to begin downloading your selected products.

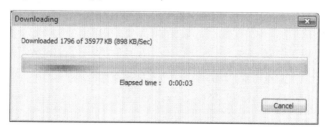

Figure 15: Stack Builder downloading applications

Once everything you selected has finished downloading, you should see the following:

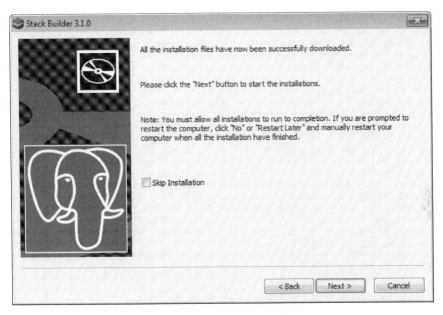

Figure 16: Stack Builder application installation

If you select the **Skip Installation** check box, Stack Builder will finish and leave the downloaded extensions in your chosen download folder. If you don't select it, the installers will run and present their own standard Windows installation processes, allowing you to set them up.

As I mentioned previously, we'll be taking a closer look at these a little later, so allow the installers to run.

The installers you do see should, like the Postgres installer, be familiar, with the usual installation choices.

Note that when you install PostGIS on one of the first screens shown, you will be asked if you would like to create a spatial database. You should answer yes to this question, as we will be using it later. PostGIS will ask you for the admin password you created previously, since the Post GIS installer will need to make changes to core database settings. Do not skip this step or use the incorrect password, as this will cause you problems later on, and may even require reinstallation.

Chapter 5 Managing Postgres and Taking Your First Steps

Postgres ships with an excellent management tool called pgAdmin. If you've followed through so far, it should have been installed with the full database product.

You should find the pgAdmin icon in the Start menu under the entry for Postgres.

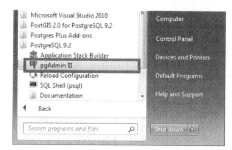

Figure 17: pgAdmin icon

If you're a bit of a command-line junkie like me, you can also use the psql command line shell. For the examples in this book we'll be using the GUI.

Click on the **pgAdmin** icon. You should be greeted with something resembling the following:

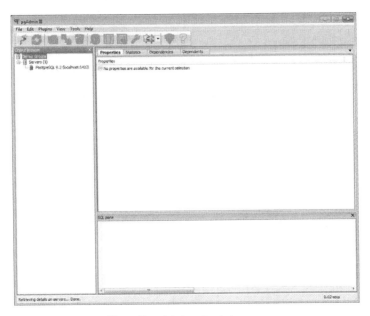

Figure 18: pgAdmin main window

As you can see, there should only be one default database instance. If you left-click on the disconnected database icon, you should see the local server statistics in the right-hand window.

Figure 19: pgAdmin local server statistics

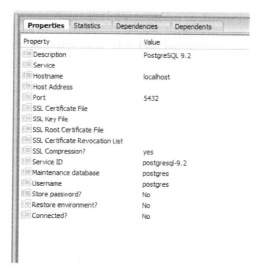

Figure 20: pgAdmin server properties

If you double-click the disconnected database icon (or right-click it and select **Connect**), you will see a password box if you selected to use a password for the Postgres account during installation.

Figure 21: pgAdmin password

Enter the password you assigned to the Postgres user account. If this is a new installation, you should have no other users in the system at this point.

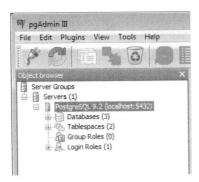

Figure 22: pgAdmin window

At this point you might find that the databases and other items available may differ, depending on what you picked at install time.

Exploring the default objects

If you installed exactly what I installed, then you should see that you have three databases, two tablespaces, no group roles, and one login role.

If you expand the databases tree, you should see the following:

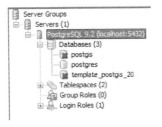

 Note: If you didn't install PostGIS, you'll only see the Postgres database listed.

The **PostGIS** database is a default database used for spatial features.

Postgres is the master database (similar to **system** in MS SQL or **MySql** in MySQL), the central database where Postgres stores all its meta information. Global tables such as **pg_catalog** and the ANSI-compatible **information_schema** aliases are stored here, along with the different configuration parameters used by any installed extensions.

Generally, you won't interact directly with this database, and you certainly are not advised to store your own user-specific data there. For the most part, access to this table is transparent, and the only time you're ever likely to reference it is when using things like the **information_schema** to gain server statistics or lists of defined objects.

The final database object is a special database type known as a template database.

Template Database

In Postgres, previously defined database structures can be left empty (devoid of data, not of objects) and then used as templates to serve as a starting point for another database.

To create a template database, you simply define the database in the same manner that you would normally, but you don't insert any data into it.

Once you have a template database, you can give specific privileges so that only certain users can use it to make new databases at new locations, enabling you to not only restrict users, but to force new databases on a server to all follow a set schema.

Where might this be useful?

Imagine teaching a class on Postgres. You could force all students to start with a known specific schema, and then control that schema so that only certain objects can be created in a specific order.

In this book we won't be going too deep into the subject, but there are entire sections devoted to it in the online manuals available at www.postgres.org.

Other objects

As noted earlier, there were a few other default objects created. Tablespaces are used by Postgres to know where in the underlying file system to store a specific database. For example, if you had a certain database that was required to be on a very fast disk, you could use a Tablespace to tell Postgres to use a specific location on a fast fiber array or high-speed storage area network (SAN), while the rest of the system resided on the same drive as the main database server. This is a whole chapter in its own right, so we won't delve in anymore than to introduce the functionality.

We also have group roles and login roles, used in the same manner as might be expected on other database systems. Group roles define access rights for entire groups of database users, while login roles define roles for single users.

If you expand the login roles tree you should see there currently exists only one user, the Postgres user. Since this user is classed as the system admin user, it's unwise to use this as your general database user. Instead, create specific users for specific databases and other objects.

As you'll see soon, Postgres security is very strict and it's very, very easy to lock yourself out of an entire cluster. Before we move on, however, there is one thing you need to be aware of if this is your first installation.

Postgres and Network Security

By default, Postgres only installs itself to be accessible from **localhost**. If you're installing this on a separate machine from the one you're working on and are setting the server up to be accessed from other workstations, you'll need to make some changes to the Postgres initialization file before you can access it. These changes are required to inform Postgres of specific IP addresses or groups of IP addresses that are expected to access this server.

If your server is not listening for connections, when you try to connect to it from a remote location you will see:

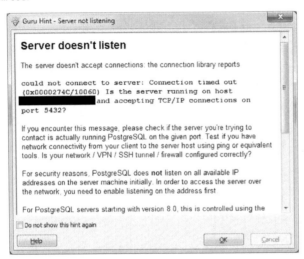

Figure 23: Postgres server not listening

Be aware that these changes are NOT based on login roles. One very common mistake I see new Postgres users make is to create login roles in order to solve this problem, and then wonder why they can't log in to the server.

To resolve this issue, you first need to be using Postgres admin on the localhost installation, so jump across via RDP or whatever method you use to the machine that you physically installed the server on, fire up, and log in to pgAdmin as shown previously.

If you scroll down in the presented dialog, it tells you to edit the Postgres configuration file. Click on the **File** menu and select **Open postgresql.conf**, which will give you a file browser to locate your master configuration file.

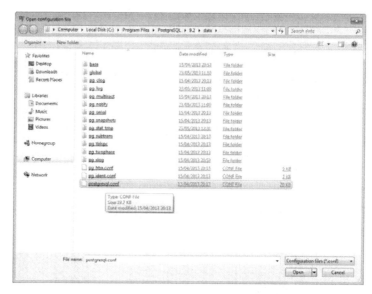

Figure 24: Open configuration file

This file usually resides in the root of your Postgres data folder. (Remember, during installation you can select the location of this separate from the server.) Once it's opened, you should see the following:

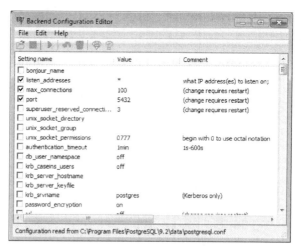

Figure 25: Backend Configuration Editor

Once you've verified that the server is listening on all IP addresses (shown by the asterisk or a specific list of IP addresses in the **listen_addresses** parameter), try to connect again. If the connection still fails, you need to check the **pg_hba.conf** file to ensure the address you wish to connect from is listed.

From the same file menu that you used to get the master Postgres configuration file, you can also open the **pg_hba** configuration file which is usually in the **data** folder alongside the master configuration file. Once you open it, you'll get the pgAdmin backend editor for that file:

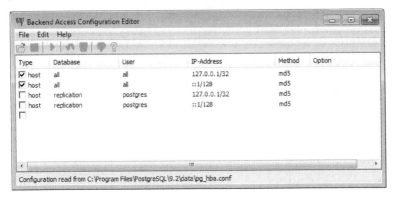

Figure 26: Backend Access Configuration Editor

As you can see, on the default server the only IP address allowed to connect is the local host address.

If you click on the blank entry at the bottom of the editor, you'll be given the option to define a new address to connect from:

Figure 27: Client Access Configuration

Select the **Enabled** option to activate this rule.

In the **Type** drop-down menu, you have the following choices:

- **local**: This is a local connection you're defining using a local socket.
- **host**: This is a remote host you're defining and the client can choose whether to use SSL.
- **hostssl**: This is a remote host you're defining and the client must use SSL to connect.
- **hostnossl**: This is a remote host you're defining and the client is never allowed to use SSL to connect.

In most cases you'll use **host** mode and leave it up to the client to decide, but it is possible to enforce SSL should you wish to.

The **Database** field allows you to set the specific database or sets of databases this rule applies to. As stated previously, Postgres security is very finely grained and you can control every aspect of access to any object in the server.

In this case, you can set things up so that certain databases can only be accessed from certain hosts. In the past I've used this to enforce web application access from a given web-server host to the database used by that application, and kept all other databases on the server secure. In practice, this means that if a web application's security was ever breached, then the only database the attacker has access to is the database used by that host. The attacker would need to gain access to other hosts or the central database server itself to access others.

As well as typing a specific database name in this box, you can also select one of the following options:

- **all**: Allow access to all databases in the server.
- **sameuser**: Allow access only to databases owned by the connecting user.
- **@<filename>**: Allow access only to named database files.
- **Samegroup**: Allow access only to databases owned by the group login being used.
- **Samerole**: Allow access only to databases owned by the user role in effect.
- **Replication**: Allow access only to the replicated version of the table and not the master.

For now, we'll just set this to **all**.

Again, as with the database box, you can type a specific user or group name in the user box, or you can use the drop-down and select **all**.

In the **IP Address** box you can specify either a single IP address or a bitmask and address combination.

Since this is a book on Postgres and not the math behind network addresses and subnet masks, I'll present a simple example. If you need to be more specific, then you'll either need to ask a friendly network administrator or find a webpage or two to read up on the subject.

If you use an IP address on your workstation of 192.168.1.10, and all the machines in your network are allocated within the 192.168.1.* range, then this is called a class C subnet. Since only the last 8-bit value in the address changes, you have a maximum of 256 hosts available (in reality, only 254 are available because 2 are usually reserved). Since a full address (all 4 numbers) is 32 bits, 32 bits minus the 8 bits for the last number leaves you with 24 bits.

If you specify your address as 192.168.1.0/24, then you're telling Postgres that any machine in the address range 192.168.1.0 through 192.168.1.255 is allowed to connect to this server.

Working out the different values and specifying them using the network forward slash notation shown previously means you can control the access of whole network clusters to the server.

Of course if you only have one PC, then putting in individual IP addresses is also valid. 192.168.1.10 would allow only the machine at this address to connect to the server.

For the purposes of this book, I'm going to select a 24-bit mask for my local network subnet.

The last option method lets you specify the connection parameters type, that is, how the password and username will be ciphered on the connection. In every case I've usually used MD5 here. You can specify others, but these are very dependent on what the underlying operating system is capable of. For example, if you select **pam** and you're running on a Linux server, then you can use the Linux Pluggable authentication module system.

Once you're done, the dialog should look similar to this:

Figure 28: Client Access Configuration

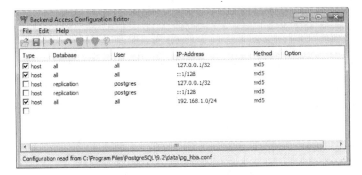

Figure 29: Backend Access Configuration Editor

Remember also that if your network uses IPv6 addresses, you will also need to define IPv6 connections, but that's beyond the scope of this book.

Once you make any changes, you'll need to restart the server and reload the configuration. You can do this from the **Start** menu option labeled **Reload Configuration**.

Figure 30: Reload Configuration

If you still have problems after reloading the configuration, try restarting the service manually using the Windows service manager. The most common reason that the settings don't reload is due to server file system permissions.

Creating your first user

Once you have everything set up to access your database server, you can move on to creating your first user. Right-click on **Login Roles** and select **New Login Role** as follows:

Figure 31: New Login Role

The following window will appear:

Figure 32: New Login Role dialog box

For an in-depth description, see the Postgres user guide. Like everything in Postgres, there is an absolute wealth under the surface that can be performed on even the simplest things. For now, enter **myuser** or some other user name you'd like to give to your new user in the **Role Name** field.

Click on the **Definition** tab to move to the password entry field:

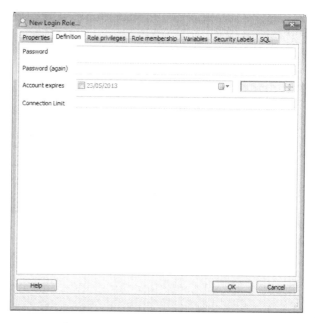

Figure 33: Definition password entry field

In the **Password** field, give your new user a password that you would like to use for connecting. In my example I will enter **myuser**, the same as the user name.

You can optionally set an expiration date for the account. I find this useful for users who are working on a contract basis, and usually set it to the end date of the contract so that on that date the account is automatically disabled. One thing to note about the expiration is that it's not like other database systems where it simply means that the password must be changed on or before that date. In Postgres, the account will be disabled after the expiration date.

You can also place a value in the **Connection Limit** field, which will allow the user only a certain number of connections before being denied. If, for example, you only wanted to allow the user to connect from one workstation using one application at a time, you would set this to a value of 1. If you leave the field empty, the number of connections for this user is unlimited.

Moving on to the **Role privileges** tab:

Figure 34: Role privileges

We're not going to change anything here, but as you can see the options are all straightforward. A point to note is that these options are server-wide and not specific to this database instance.

The next tab, **Role membership**, allows you to allocate this user to different login groups. Since we won't be using those in this book, I'll leave you explore that one at your own leisure.

The **Variables** and **Security Labels** tabs are used in advanced situations; again this is beyond the scope of this book and won't be covered. The last tab, **SQL**, simply shows you the SQL statements that will be generated to create this user.

Once you've finished, click **OK** to add your user, and the user should appear in the **Login Roles** tree:

Figure 35: New user in Login Roles

Now that you have a user, let's create a database.

Creating your first database

If you right-click on the **Databases** tree and select **New Database**, you should see a tabbed window similar to the one for adding a new user:

Figure 36: New Database window

On the first tab, we'll name the new database **mydatabase** and select the new user we just created from the **Owner** drop-down list. If you wish, you can also add a comment in the **Comment** field.

Before we go further, there is a very important point that we need to cover regarding object names in Postgres, and it's one that always trips up new users.

Postgres object names are case sensitive

If you create two tables called **MyTable** and **mytable**, you will create two database tables with unique names.

You might be wondering why this creates problems. Well, when you reference an object name in a SQL statement, Postgres automatically makes that object name lowercase.

For example, if you were to type `select * from MyTable` in the pgAdmin SQL editor, Postgres would actually try to execute `select * from mytable`, which as you can see, would give you the wrong data from the wrong table.

Why on earth would you do that? Most of the architectures that Postgres was originally written for all have case sensitive file systems, and so originally this wasn't a problem—whatever you typed in was interpreted exactly as you typed it.

Then Postgres was ported to systems such as Windows, and the problem of dealing with non-case-sensitive file systems arose. The development team had to find a way to not break existing compatibility while ensuring that something like unintentional file-overwriting did not happen.

How was this addressed? As I've already explained, newer versions of Postgres now by default spell object names in lowercase regardless of how you type them in a SQL statement. If you want to force the name to be used exactly as typed, then you need to surround the name with double quotes.

Going back to our last example, using `select * from "MyTable"` will select the correct table, while using any of the following will select the second table as the target:

```
select * from mytable
```

```
select * from MyTable
```

```
select * from MYTABLE
```

```
select * from "mytable"
```

When you specify names and object attributes in any of the dialogs in pgAdmin, these names are automatically double quoted, so if you specify MyTable in a GUI dialog and then mistakenly type `select * from MyTable` in the SQL editor, you'll likely find that it doesn't work as expected.

Continuing with our new table

The best practice in the Postgres community is to make all your object names, tables, columns, users, etc., lowercase, or ensure that you wrap every access in double quotes before using them. I personally always use the first method; once you've typed half a dozen spatial SQL statements and had to double quote them throughout, you'll soon realize just how complicated it can get.

Enter a name for your new database, choose an owner, and click on the **Definition** tab.

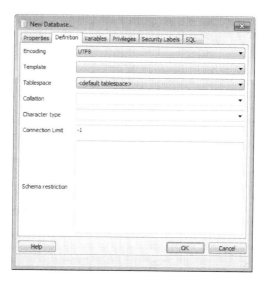

Figure 37: New Database window

For the most part you can leave the encoding option as the default, but you may want to change it if you're going to support Unicode, Kanji, or some other type of font mapping. I've never had any issues using UTF8.

The **Template** drop-down allows you to pick a template database on which to base this new database. As previously mentioned, this allows you to enforce a specific database setup. For now, leave this blank.

You should also leave the **Tablespace** and other options set to default unless you have a reason to change them.

For this exercise we will not be using anything on any of the other tabs since most are only needed in specific circumstances. For a general database it's usually enough to set the name, user, and if you're using one, a template name.

Once you click **OK**, your new database should appear in the **Databases** list.

Figure 38: Object browser

Congratulations, you now have your first Postgres database. You can now start to create tables and store data in it just as you do with any other database system.

Before we move on to the next chapter, we'll create a new table to experiment with.

Expand the tree below your new database until you see the **Tables** tree, and then right-click on **Tables** and select **New Table**.

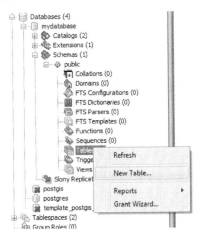

Figure 39: Select New Table

The window that opens is similar to those we've seen so far, with the same options on the same tabs and generally in the same order.

In the **Properties** tab, enter a name, choose your user, and enter a comment (optional):

Figure 40: Properties tab

Switch to the **Columns** tab so we can start to add columns to the table.

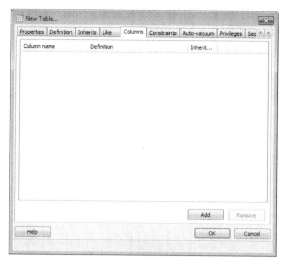

Figure 41: Columns tab

Click **Add** to add your first column:

Figure 42: New Column

The first column we're going to add is a primary integer record key, with an Identity.

As I've pointed out previously, there are many questions that .NET programmers familiar with MS SQL ask, and creating an **Identity** column is another of those issues for new Postgres users.

Postgres does have automatically incrementing columns, but they are handled differently than other databases. In MS SQL for example, you add an **Identity** attribute to the column, while in MySQL you add an **autoincrement** attribute.

In Postgres, however, any column type can be made to automatically increment no matter what the data type is. For example, you could have a text column with **File1**, **File2**, **File3**, and so on.

Postgres does this by associating a **Sequence** with the column in question, and then assigning the **Sequence** to the default value. You can do this by hand if you wish (and in some cases you will need to, especially for custom data types), but if all you're using is an integer, Postgres makes it easy by providing a custom data type alias called **serial**.

Give our column a name (**gid** is typical of the name used for an ID column in Postgres), and select **serial** from the **Data type** drop-down list.

We won't change anything on the other tabs for now, but do by all means have a look and see what's there. On the **Privileges** tab for example, you might be surprised to see that Postgres security is so controllable that you can actually mark individual columns in a table to be used only by specific users.

Click **OK** and that column will now be added to your table. Don't worry about the primary key; we'll add that in just a moment.

Let's add the following columns:

name	character varying	50
email	character varying	50
webpage	character varying	100
bio	text	n/a

Don't forget the notes on case sensitivity from earlier!

You should now have a table that looks like the following:

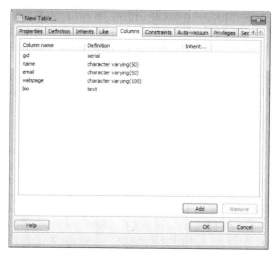

Figure 43: New Table

Now we'll add our primary key. Click on the **Constraints** tab.

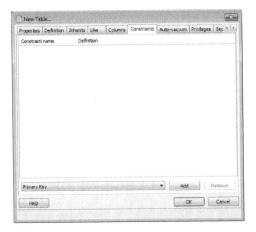

Figure 44: Constraints tab

Make sure **Primary Key** is selected in the drop-down menu at the bottom of the page, and then click **Add**. You should see the following:

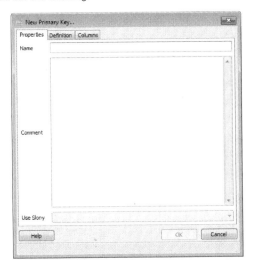

Figure 45: New Primary Key

We'll call our key **pk_gid_people**. Type the key name in the name field then click on the **Columns** tab. Select the **gid** column from the column drop-down list and click **Add**. You should end up with the following:

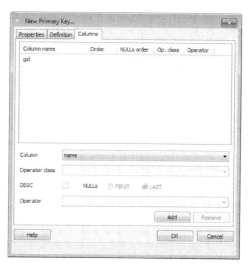

Figure 46: Add columns

You can add as many columns as you want to the primary key from here, and then repeat the process to add further indexes from the many different types available on as many columns as you need. This is also where you would create foreign key relations to maintain referential integrity in the database between linked records.

For now, click **OK**.

Once you're back at the table definition dialog box, click **OK** to create and save the table.

Your table will appear in the right-hand pane:

Figure 47: New table

You now have a basic Postgres table, database, and user to start playing with. Close pgAdmin and return to the desktop. In the next chapter we'll start from scratch and log in with our normal user account.

Chapter 6 Basic SQL

Compared to the other chapters in this book, this will be a reasonably short one. Why?

Well it's very simple really. Postgres is 100 percent ANSI-95 and beyond SQL compliant.

What this means in practice is that everything you already know about your existing database of choice that is standard compatible SQL will still work in Postgres.

There are already many excellent SQL references available on the Internet, so it would be of no use for me to cover stuff that's already done better elsewhere.

Getting your SQL commands into Postgres is typically done in one of two ways. For one, you can use pgAdmin's SQL editor where you get syntax highlighting and full-screen editing. You can open this by selecting the database node in the object tree that you wish to work with, and then clicking on the SQL magnifying glass button on the main toolbar:

Figure 48: SQL editor button

This will open the following editor for you to enter your SQL queries:

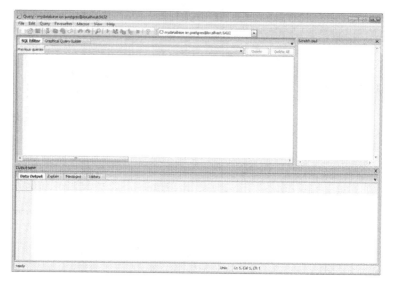

Figure 49: SQL Editor

Or you can choose the **Graphical Query Builder** tab:

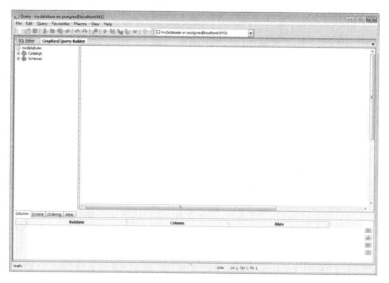

Figure 50: Graphical Query Builder

The other way is to execute the **SQL Shell** option from the Postgres group in your Windows **Start** menu:

Figure 51: Postgres in Start menu

When selecting this option you'll be prompted to enter information such as server address, database name, user name, and password. You should end up with something like the following if you use the objects we created in the last chapter:

```
SQL Shell (psql)
Server [localhost]:
Database [postgres]: mydatabase
Port [5432]:
Username [postgres]: myuser
Password for user myuser:
psql (9.2.4)
WARNING: Console code page (850) differs from Windows code page (1252)
         8-bit characters might not work correctly. See psql reference
         page "Notes for Windows users" for details.
Type "help" for help.

mydatabase=> _
```

Figure 52: SQL Shell

The commands that the shell recognizes can be found at http://www.postgresql.org/docs/9.0/static/app-psql.html.

I won't repeat them all here, as we'll be using the GUI, but if you need to script your interactions with Postgres, then the PSQL shell is the perfect way to do so. If you're logged in and can't find a way out, **\q** will quit the shell.

Putting in the practice

Open a pgAdmin and click on the magnifying glass icon shown in Figure 48 to open the SQL editor.

I often find it's useful to expand the tree for the tables I'm working with, and then resize my **Query** window so it covers the right-hand pane as shown in the following figure:

Figure 53: Resizing the Query window

This allows me to see my table and column names and such while I'm typing so that I can see what I'm working with.

First we'll insert some data into our test table. Type the following into your SQL window, and then click the **Run** button or press F5 to execute it.

```
insert into

mytable(name, email, webpage, bio)

values(

  "Peter Shaw",

  "shawty_ds@yahoo.com",

  "http://shawtyds.wordpress.com",

  "a Geek pure and simple....")
```

If you've done this, then you'll be looking at an error message and wondering why a column with the same name as the first field's data doesn't exist.

Remember what I was saying earlier about case sensitivity in object names? Well, if you look I made the classic mistake of using double quotes when entering strings.

Like much of the advice I've given so far, this is another sticking point that frequently catches new users of Postgres. While I agree the error message could be better, Postgres is actually doing what it's supposed to and trying to interpret the table or object name as it's spelled.

If you change all those double quotes to single, then you should see that the new row is now inserted into your table.

Repeat the command a few times with different data just so you have four or five more rows of data to play with.

You'll notice that when applying the **insert** command, we specifically told Postgres exactly what columns we wanted to insert by including a comma list in brackets after the table name, and we made sure that exactly the same number of data parameters were provided in the values portion.

This was done so that we would not attempt to insert data into the **gid** column, which if you remember, is now under the control of a Postgres sequence.

If you now type:

```
select * from mytable
```

into the SQL editor and press F5, then you should see something like the following, only showing the data you inserted instead:

Figure 54: Output pane

Other simple SQL statements work as you would expect:

```
select * from mytable where gid = 2
```

	gid integer	name character varying(50)	email character varying(50)	webpage character varying(100)	bio text
1	2	Peter Shaw 2	shawty ds@yahoo.co	http://shawtyds.wor	a Ge

Figure 55: Output pane

```
select * from mytable where gid in(2,3,4)
```

	gid integer	name character varying(50)	email character varying(50)	webpage character varying(100)	bio text
1	2	Peter Shaw 2	shawty ds@yahoo.co	http://shawtyds.wor	a Ge
2	3	Peter Shaw 3	shawty ds@yahoo.co	http://shawtyds.wor	a Ge
3	4	Peter Shaw 4	shawty ds@yahoo.co	http://shawtyds.wor	a Ge

Figure 56: Output pane

```
update mytable set name = 'Alan Person' where gid = 3
```

Query returned successfully: one row affected, 15 ms execution time.

Figure 57: Output pane

	gid integer	name character varying(50)	email character varying(50)	webpage character varying(100)	bio text
1	1	Peter Shaw	shawty ds@yahoo.co	http://shawtyds.wor	a Ge
2	2	Peter Shaw 2	shawty ds@yahoo.co	http://shawtyds.wor	a Ge
3	4	Peter Shaw 4	shawty ds@yahoo.co	http://shawtyds.wor	a Ge
4	5	Peter Shaw 5	shawty ds@yahoo.co	http://shawtyds.wor	a Ge
5	3	Alan Person	shawty ds@yahoo.co	http://shawtyds.wor	a Ge

Figure 58: Output pane

```
delete from mytable where gid = 4
```

Figure 59: Output pane

gid integer	name character varying(50)	email character varying(50)	webpage character varying(100)	bio text
1	1	Peter Shaw	shawty ds@yahoo.co	http://shawtyds.wor	a Ge
2	2	Peter Shaw 2	shawty ds@yahoo.co	http://shawtyds.wor	a Ge
3	5	Peter Shaw 5	shawty ds@yahoo.co	http://shawtyds.wor	a Ge
4	3	Alan Person	shawty ds@yahoo.co	http://shawtyds.wor	a Ge

Figure 60: Output pane

One more thing before we move on: Because Postgres is so compatible, querying the **INFORMATION_SCHEMA** table the same way you do in many other database systems will yield the same results.

```
SELECT * FROM information_schema.columns
```

When run on MS SQL using SQL Management Studio, and on Postgres using pgAdmin, this command returns the same columns of information:

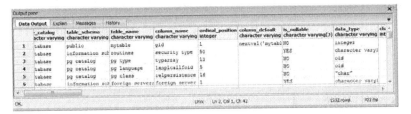

Figure 61: Output pane

In the next chapter we'll cover some more interesting examples of SQL that are specific to Postgres.

Chapter 7 Postgres-Specific SQL

In this chapter we'll look at some of the SQL commands that can only be found in Postgres. There will be some overlap between Postgres and other database systems, and all services do in some way have their own methods of achieving some of the things we'll be looking at here. However, I'll be picking things that are specific to Postgres, and even if they are available on other platforms, I've picked them mainly because Postgres performs them so well that I would never consider using another platform or database engine to work with that feature.

Let's kick off with…

Data Type Conversion

All database engines can convert from one data type to another. It's a required process since database engines are designed to handle various types of data.

If all databases have to handle this functionality, then why is Postgres so special?

Well, most databases implement data conversion in a very long-winded way. Assuming that we have a table with an integer column and a timestamp column in it, let me show you what I mean:

```
SELECT CAST(column1 AS varchar(30)), CAST(column2 AS DATE) FROM mytable;
```

This statement will select the values in **column1** and **column2** from a table called **mytable**, and in the process it will use the **cast** function to convert the value to a **varchar(30)** and a date at the same time.

To most developers this is not really a problem; it's the norm. We nest functions, and we string things together in a fluent manner, so seeing something like the previous statement really doesn't shock us.

Unfortunately to many developers, the previous code is rather messy and hard to maintain. The authors of Postgres knew this, so they decided to add this functionality a different way:

```
SELECT column1::varchar(30), column2::date FROM mytable;
```

As you can see, this statement reads much easier than the first one. It's also more intuitive and easy to recognize exactly what's going on.

This on-the-fly data conversion is not restricted to **SELECT** either; you can also use it with **INSERT**:

```
INSERT INTO mytable(column1, column2) VALUES('100'::integer, '2013-05-
30T19:30'::timestamp)
```

The same is also true for functions:

```
SELECT myfunction(column1::varchar(30))
```

Anywhere you would use a normal column or variable specification in your queries, you can use data type casting to convert values on-the-fly.

There is one thing to notice though—it's not magic. For example, it will still create an error if you try to convert "hello" to an integer, but as long as you're handling errors in some fashion, then you can watch for and handle this scenario.

The Postgres manual page detailing this can be found at:

http://www.postgresql.org/docs/9.2/static/sql-expressions.html#SQL-SYNTAX-TYPE-CASTS

Data Validation Constraints

How many times have you had to write the same boilerplate business logic to make sure that a set of values fall into the same range?

Take for example two product price values.

These values would generally be represented by a standard decimal number value, one might be a full price, and another might be a discounted price.

In each case the standard data types will still allow negative numbers, and without business logic in your application code, you can't enforce the discount code to always be a lesser value than the full price.

Postgres can solve these problems directly in the database by using something called a check constraint.

Check constraints are defined at table creation time, just like normal SQL constraints such as **not null**. Taking our price example, we could define a table as follows (there is no need to enter this right now; it's for illustration against regular SQL only):

```
create table pricetable(

    record_id serial primary key,
```

```
    fullprice number(12,2),

    discountprice number(12,2)
);
```

As you can see, there's nothing special about it; it's a simple table definition.

If we now rewrite our DDL to enforce our rules:

```
create table pricetable(

    record_id serial primary key,

    fullprice number(12,2) check(fullprice > 0),

    discountprice number(12,2) check(discountprice > 0 AND discountprice <
fullprice)
);
```

You'll see that it's as simple as adding a check to the column definition line.

Just by adding those two simple check constraints to our table, we've now enforced those business rules directly on our table. Postgres will now refuse to allow data that violates these business rules to be inserted into this table.

We can also go one step further.

The checks we've added are known as column checks, and will be evaluated only when there is a change on that particular column. You can also specify that a check be placed on the table itself.

```
create table pricetable(

    record_id serial primary key,

    fullprice numeric(12,2) check(fullprice > 0),

    discountprice numeric(12,2) check(discountprice > 0),

    check(discountprice < fullprice)
);
```

When you add a check to a table in this manner, that check is evaluated when any column in the table is updated, not just the column that the check is attached to.

Taking our example, any time **fullprice** is changed or has a value inserted, it's checked to make sure that it is greater than 0. The same is also true for discount price. The discount < full is evaluated even if **record_id** is changed, meaning no matter the update, your data integrity is always re-evaluated.

Checks can also do some complex math across multiple columns.

Take the following example:

```
create table people(

    id bigint primary key,

    first character varying(100) not null,

    last character varying(100),

    email character varying(200),

    dateofbirth date not null

)
```

This is another fairly typical table definition, again nothing special. However, if we now add the following table level check:

```
create table people(

    id bigint primary key,

    first character varying(100) not null,

    last character varying(100),

    email character varying(200),

    dateofbirth date not null,

    check(

        DATE_PART('year', dateofbirth::timestamp) <

        DATE_PART('year', now() - interval '18 years')

    )
```

```
)
```

You have a self-validating table that won't allow you to add or change a date of birth such that a person becomes 18 years of age or younger.

You wouldn't rely on this in its entirety. Someone, for example, could easily lie about his or her date of birth among other things, but you begin to see how you can easily start to add an extra layer of validation into your applications.

Check constraints can use any combination of variables, column data, custom functions, and anything else available to a normal SQL query. The only limit in how you combine them is your imagination.

You can find the manual page about data validation constraints at http://www.postgresql.org/docs/9.2/static/ddl-constraints.html.

Postgres Arrays

I've mentioned Postgres array handling a couple of times already, but now it's time to show it off a little bit.

Many database purists would argue that having the capability to put multiple values in a single value field is a bad design decision, and in many cases it does detract from the nature of having fully normalized rows of data in well-designed tables.

However, there are some cases where these multi-value fields can be useful. The thing to remember as I go through this next section is that this is just another tool in the Postgres toolkit.

You don't have to use arrays if they don't solve the problem you're trying to solve; it's up to you to decide if they are the right tool for the job.

Like much of the Postgres extended functionality, arrays are defined at table creation time. You can use any of the Postgres types available and turn it into an array just by adding square brackets to the data type.

Take the following example:

```
create table lotterynumbers(

    name character varying(50),

    numbers integer[]

)

If you've inserted this statement, then be aware running the next statement
immediately after will give you an error due to the table name being the same. You
```

The **name** column is just a standard string, and the **numbers** column is an array of undefined length. If we wanted to make the array a fixed size, we simply add that size to the table definition:

```
create table lotterynumbers(

        name character varying(50),

        numbers integer[6]

)
```

Now only six integers can be stored in the field.

Once the table has been defined, you can populate it as follows:

```
insert into lotterynumbers(name, numbers) values('peter', { 1,2,3,4,5,6 })
```

Once you have data in an array field, you can easily access it using an index (in a very similar fashion to .NET and many other languages). Something to note here: In my example insert, you'll see that I don't enclose the {} array specification in single quotes. This is the way it's always worked as far as I'm aware. The version (v9.0) that I'm testing this on accepts the line without the quotes, but it appears that newer versions do not.

If you get a syntax error while trying the inserted code, then try repeating it with single quotes around the array specification as follows:

```
insert into lotterynumbers(name, numbers) values('peter', '{ 1,2,3,4,5,6 }')
```

Also keep this in mind for future statements using array syntax from this point on. If you get a syntax error, try using single quotes around the specifier.

To get back only the first lottery number:

```
select name,numbers[1] from lotterynumbers
```

You can also select a slice of the array:

```
select name,numbers[3:4] from lotterynumbers
```

Just as you can select by index, you can also update individual indexes:

```
update lotterynumbers set numbers[5] = 50;
```

And again, you can also use slices:

```
update lotterynumbers set numbers[2:3] = { 7,8 };
```

Replacing the entire array is just as easy:

```
update lotterynumbers set numbers = { 9,8,7,6,5,4 };
```

If you haven't set any limits on the array, then you can arbitrarily extend it by using the concatenation operator:

```
update lotterynumbers set numbers = numbers || { 8,9,10 }
```

As well as the previous examples, you can easily perform array-wide searches.

If you have a fixed-size array, you can do the following:

```
select * from lotterynumbers where numbers[1] = 10 and numbers[6] = 20
```

If you have a bigger array, or your array is not a fixed size, you can use the **ANY** operator, which behaves exactly like the .NET **ANY** operator in LINQ in that any array element that contains the desired check will be returned.

```
select * from lotterynumbers where 20 = ANY(numbers)
```

Notice that the syntax is not quite what you might expect. It's done this way because you're actually looking to see if anything in the array matches your criteria, as opposed to looking in the array to see if it contains your criteria.

If you suspect that more than one element in your array will contain the value you are looking for, then you can have Postgres return all matches as a subarray using the **ALL** operator:

```
select * from lotterynumbers where 20 = ALL(numbers)
```

You can find much more detailed information, including how to use second and third arrays and negative indexes, on the Postgres manual page at http://www.postgresql.org/docs/9.2/static/arrays.html.

Please note that I've linked the 9.2 version. You may need to adjust the version number to get the correct page.

Inherited Tables

Inherited tables are very simple; so simple, in fact, that you don't actually need to learn anything new to use them other than a single keyword.

Just like with many other unique Postgres features, everything is built on standard SQL constructs. Let's use the idea discussed in previous chapters, and show the SQL that might be used to construct our staff tables. First, our master table:

```
create table staff(

        fullname character varying(100) not null,

        wageband character varying(25) not null,

        phonenumber character varying(10),

        department character varying(25) not null

)
```

Like many other examples, it's a standard bit of DDL. In .NET, this would be the base class. We would then inherit our other tables from it:

```
create table itstaff(

        languages character varying(50)[],
```

```
        coursestaken character varying(50)[],

        currentproject character varying(25),

        systemowned character varying(25)

) inherits(staff)

create table accountsstaff(

        projectsowned character varying(50)[],

        clientsresponsiblefor int[],

        subdepartment int,

        officename character varying(50)

) inherits(staff)
```

If you now use **select** on those tables, you should see the following:

```
select * from itstaff
```

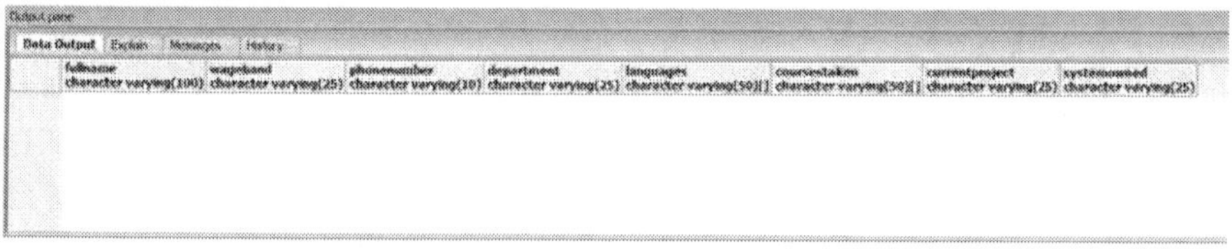

fullname character varying(100)	wageband character varying(25)	phonenumber character varying(10)	department character varying(25)	languages character varying(50)[]	coursestaken character varying(50)[]	currentproject character varying(25)	systemowned character varying(25)

Figure 62: Output pane

```
select * from accountsstaff
```

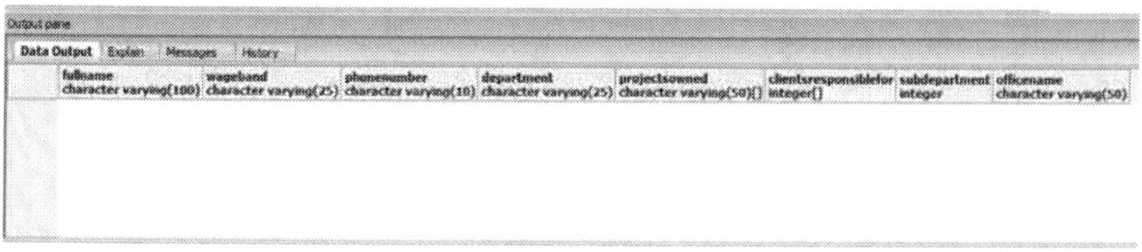

fullname character varying(100)	wageband character varying(25)	phonenumber character varying(10)	department character varying(25)	projectsowned character varying(50)[]	clientsresponsiblefor integer[]	subdepartment integer	officename character varying(50)

Figure 63: Output pane

You can see immediately that both tables have the same columns as the staff table, as well as the extra columns that were added in each of their own definitions.

Data is also inherited but not quite in the way you might think.

Inserts in the parent table do not show up in the child tables. It's a common misconception to those new to inheritance in Postgres that this is the case.

Data is ONLY inherited up the tree, not down it, so in this case inserting data into **staff** will not be visible in the **itstaff** or **accountsstaff** tables:

```
insert into staff values(

'Peter Shaw', 'A', '0123456789', 'Technical'

)

select * from staff
```

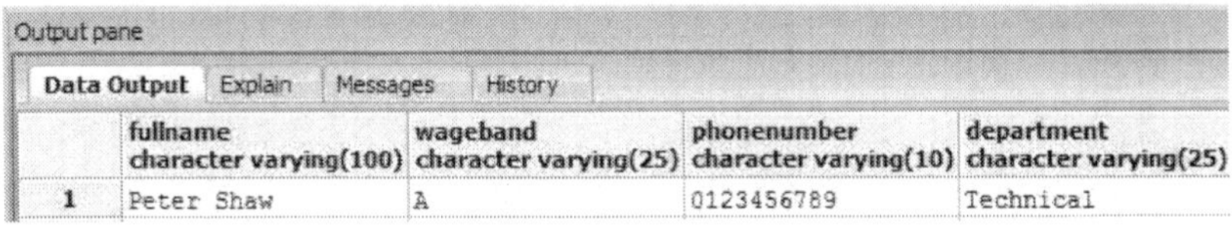

	fullname character varying(100)	wageband character varying(25)	phonenumber character varying(10)	department character varying(25)
1	Peter Shaw	A	0123456789	Technical

Figure 64: Output pane

```
select * from itstaff
```

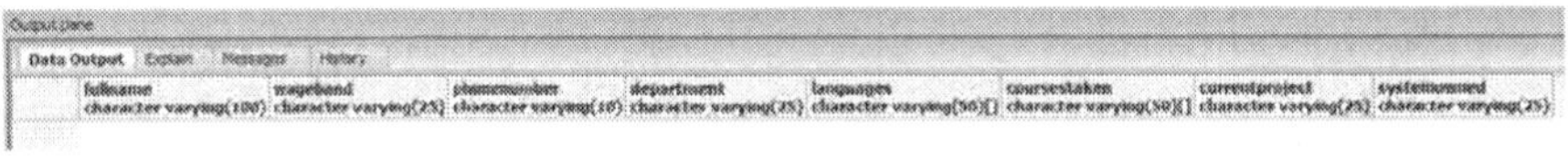

Figure 65: Output pane

```
select * from accountsstaff
```

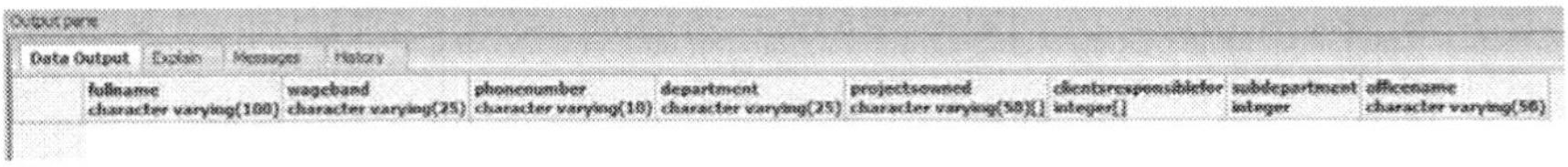

Figure 66: Output pane

However, because data propagates up the tree, performing the following:

```
insert into itstaff values(

'Peter Shaw 2', 'B', '', 'Development', '{C, Pascal, C++, C#, PHP}','{dev1, dev2,
dev3}','Postgres Book','DS'

)
```

results in this:

```
select * from itstaff
```

Figure 67: Output pane

```
select * from staff
```

	fullname character varying(100)	wageband character varying(25)	phonenumber character varying(10)	department character varying(25)
1	Peter Shaw	A	0123456789	Technical
2	Peter Shaw 2	B		Development

Figure 68: Output pane

This also applies to the **accountsstaff** table:

```
insert into accountsstaff values(

'Peter Shaw 3', 'C', '', 'Admin', '{proj1, proj2, proj3}','{1, 2, 3}',20,'North
Durham'

)

select * from accountsstaff
```

Figure 69: Output pane

```
select * from staff
```

fullname character varying(100)	wageband character varying(25)	phonenumber character varying(10)	department character varying(25)
1	Peter Shaw	A	0123456789	Technical
2	Peter Shaw 2	B		Development
3	Peter Shaw 3	C		Admin

Figure 70: Output pane

As you can see, this could potentially be very useful in some situations. You most likely would not use the parent table for most data modification operations, but you might in theory use it for reporting.

A read-only table that has every staff member in the organization in it, for example, is much easier to read and perform reports against than several separate tables.

The departments responsible for each type of employee can then update and keep their own data in order without causing problems for the others.

Note also that there is no sideways manipulation; that is, a record added and maintained in the **accountsstaff** table is not visible in the **itstaff** table and vice versa.

Another added advantage is that any schema changes made to the parent table are instantly replicated to inherited tables.

If we add a new column to our staff table:

```
alter table staff add column age integer;

select * from staff
```

we get:

	fullname character varying(100)	wageband character varying(25)	phonenumber character varying(10)	department character varying(25)	age integer
1	Peter Shaw	A	0123456789	Technical	
2	Peter Shaw 2	B		Development	
3	Peter Shaw 3	C		Admin	

Figure 71: Output pane

And then going on to do:

```
select * from itstaff
```

and

```
select * from accountsstaff
```

we get:

Figure 72: Output pane

and

Figure 73: Output pane

Both changes are instantly useable as described previously, so updating the age in the child tables will show up in the parent tables.

There is one instance where data changes in the parent table do show up in the child tables, and that is if you change data that was inserted into the database using a child table.

Take the following example:

```
select * from staff
```

	fullname character varying(100)	wageband character varying(25)	phonenumber character varying(10)	department character varying(25)	age integer
1	Peter Shaw	A	0123456789	Technical	
2	Peter Shaw 2	B		Development	
3	Peter Shaw 3	C		Admin	

Figure 74: Output pane

Peter Shaw 2 shows up because it was inserted as part of the record in **itstaff**. If we update that as follows:

```
update staff set age = 21 where fullname = 'Peter Shaw 2'

select * from staff
```

Output pane

	fullname character varying(100)	wageband character varying(25)	phonenumber character varying(10)	department character varying(25)	age integer
1	Peter Shaw	A	0123456789	Technical	
2	Peter Shaw 2	B		Development	21
3	Peter Shaw 3	C		Admin	

Figure 75: Output pane

And then also perform:

```
select * from itstaff
```

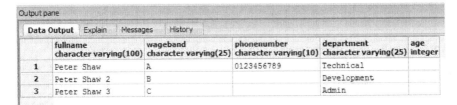

	fullname character varying(100)	wageband character varying(25)	phonenumber character varying(10)	department character varying(25)	languages character varying(50)[]	coursestaken character varying(50)[]	currentproject character varying(25)[]	systemowned character varying(25)	age integer
1	Peter Shaw 2	B		Development	{C, Pascal, C++, C#, PHP}	{dev1, dev2, dev3}	Postgres Book	OS	21

Figure 76: Output pane

We can see that the data has propagated down.

This shouldn't be a surprise though. It makes sense that anything created elsewhere, and that can be modified elsewhere, would show up in different places.

It does mean, however, that when you design databases using inherited tables, you absolutely must make sure you have your designs properly planned out beforehand.

If you're a software developer who is accustomed to using strict object-oriented principles, then what you've just done here will likely make a lot of sense. Postgres is a database that's very strong on object-oriented design and allows you to treat data stores just as you would treat objects in a software application.

Using inheritance is a very powerful tool, but can also cause a lot of problems that can be hard to diagnose. I know because I'm usually the one diagnosing them.

The section on table inheritance in the Postgres manual can be found at http://www.postgresql.org/docs/9.2/static/ddl-inherit.html.

Processing XML Data

Every database has some form of XML processing built into it, and most of them are horribly complicated. Postgres, on the other hand, makes handling XML simple with a slew of very easy-to-use XML construction functions.

It also natively supports an XML data type, and can insert XML data directly into a database field and then perform queries directly on that XML data using **XPath**. We'll cover that later.

To create data suitable for an XML field in a database table, use the **xmlparse** function, which parses XML character data and returns an XML data type.

Xmlparse takes two parameters, one describing the scope of the generated XML string, and the other the XML data itself. Note, however, that **xmlparse** is defined in the SQL 2008 standards document. In typical fashion, Postgres has its own way of performing the deed with simpler syntax, as well as supporting the standards.

```
xml '<tag>tagvalue</tag>'
```

or

```
'<tag>tagvalue</tag>'
```

I'll use the Postgres syntax for the rest of this section. If you want to read up on how to use **xmlparse** you can do so on the XML data type page in the Postgres manual at http://www.postgresql.org/docs/9.2/static/datatype-xml.html.

Here is a quick example for those who want one to try now:

```
XMLPARSE (CONTENT 'abc<foo>bar</foo><bar>foo</bar>')
```

You can change **CONTENT** for **DOCUMENT** and the output XML will then also include a valid XML document type declaration.

The inverse operation is the **xmlserialize** function, which returns a character string value from an XML data type as follows:

```
select xmlserialize(CONTENT 'tagvalue'::xml as character varying)
```

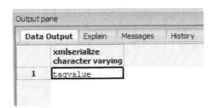

*Figure 77: The **xmlserialize** function*

The **xmlserialize** function takes a Postgres XML data type and converts it back into a standard XML string, unlike the preceding **xmlparse** statement which takes a standard XML formatted string and parses it into an XML data type. Using the two together (or the simplified syntax if you prefer) is the key to getting XML data into and out of a Postgres database in its own native XML storage type. You'll also notice that both of them can take either a **CONTENT** or **DOCUMENT** keyword. The difference is that **DOCUMENT** will produce XML output that has a full document type header attached to it, whereas **CONTENT** will not.

If your intention is to produce XML that will be saved to a stand-alone XML data file, then you should use **DOCUMENT** to ensure that you attach any extra information required by the target. If you're producing snippets of XML to be inserted inline in another document, or if you're producing XML that will be output by an XML web service, then **CONTENT** is more appropriate.

You might notice that in the previous example, there are no XML tags in the text passed to **xmlserialize**.

The reason for this is even when you parse a value out of the string, it still gets presented as an XML data type. Generally you would use **XPath** to grab the value you need, and then **xmlserialize** to convert it to the correct type.

A word of warning though: the XML data type doesn't validate using DTDs or XML Schema documents; it is possible to put malformed XML into XML fields if you're not careful.

Once you master using the XML data type, you can move on to using the rich set of XML functions available. I'm not going to cover all of them in this book, just the basics. You can find the whole list of them along with examples at http://www.postgresql.org/docs/9.2/static/functions-xml.html.

The first thing we're going to look at is producing XML data from data stored in your database tables.

If you've been reading from the beginning, you'll recall that previously we created a table called **mytable**. It looks like the following:

```
select * from mytable
```

Figure 78: mytable

We'll be using this for our XML sample in just a moment.

All of the Postgres XML functions start with **xml**, and all of them build on previous functionality provided by the others.

Starting with something simple, we have **xmlcomment**:

```
select xmlcomment('This is a comment')
```

This will produce the following:

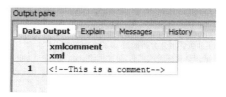

Figure 79: xmlcomment

Following that, we have **xmlconcat**, which concatenates two discrete bits of XML data together to form one. Note that it does not nest elements.

```
select xmlconcat('<tag>Hello</tag>','<tag>World</tag>')
```

Figure 80: xmlconcat

Just like everywhere else in Postgres, you can nest these functions too:

```
select xmlconcat(xmlcomment('This is a comment'),'<tag>Hello World</tag>')
```

Figure 81: xmlconcat

The next function, and the one you are most likely to use very often, is **xmlelement**. This function allows you to construct elements from raw data like so:

```
select xmlelement(name tag, 'Hello World')
```

Figure 82: xmlelement

Like the others, it can be easily nested:

```
select xmlconcat(xmlcomment('This is a comment'), xmlelement(name tag, 'Hello World'))
```

Figure 83: xmlelement

The **xmlelement** function can also be nested inside other xmlelements, and when you start to do this, you start to be able to nest and wrap XML tags:

```
select

    xmlelement(name outertag,

        xmlelement(name innertag, 'tagvalue')

    )
```

Figure 84: xmlelement

Going one step further, **xmlelement** can nest multiple recurrences:

```
select

    xmlelement(name outertag,

        xmlelement(name innertag1, 'tagvalue'),

        xmlelement(name innertag2, 'tagvalue')

    )
```

Figure 85: xmlelement

So how do you use this to export tables to XML? Quite simply: Wrap multiple **xmlelements** into a select that selects the table data you wish to export using another function, **xmlagg**.

```
select

        xmlelement(name users,

            xmlagg(

                xmlelement(name user,

                    xmlelement(name gid, gid),

                    xmlelement(name name, name),

                    xmlelement(name email, email),

                    xmlelement(name webpage, webpage)

                )

            )

        )

from mytable
```

The **xmlagg** function is slightly different than the other XML functions. Its purpose, very much like the aggregate functions in general, is to take multiple generated rows from a select query and aggregate them into one XML data row.

As can be seen in the previous example, **xmlagg** takes the multiple rows of output produced by the inner **xmlelement** call, and then aggregates them into one set of XML tags representing the whole table, before one final **xmlelement** call is used to wrap each row in an outer **users** tag. The result is the following XML, which I've formatted into multiple lines for readability.

Make a note of this XML output; we'll be using it later when we read an XML file back into your Postgres server. You can **Copy** and **Paste** it into a file called **users.xml** to make it ready for later use.

```xml
<users>

    <user>

        <gid>1</gid>

        <name>Peter Shaw</name>

        <email>shawty_ds@yahoo.com</email>

        <webpage>http://shawtyds.wordpress.com</webpage>

    </user>

    <user>

        <gid>2</gid>

        <name>Peter Shaw 2</name>

        <email>shawty_ds@yahoo.com</email>

        <webpage>http://shawtyds.wordpress.com</webpage>

    </user>

    <user>

        <gid>5</gid>

        <name>Peter Shaw 5</name>

        <email>shawty_ds@yahoo.com</email>

        <webpage>http://shawtyds.wordpress.com</webpage>

    </user>

    <user>

        <gid>3</gid>

        <name>Alan Person</name>

        <email>shawty_ds@yahoo.com</email>

        <webpage>http://shawtyds.wordpress.com</webpage>
```

```
        </user>
</users>
```

Postgres also has one quicker way to export your entire table to XML, **table_to_xml**.

```
select table_to_xml('mytable',TRUE,TRUE,'')
```

Figure 86: table_to_xml

I'm not going to cover the different options here, but by changing them you can change the layout of the XML quite substantially. They are documented on the manual page listed previously (http://www.postgresql.org/docs/9.2/static/functions-xml.html), along with similar functions that will generate DTD and schema documents for your XML based on the original SQL used to create your table.

That leaves us with one last question...

How do you get your XML data back into Postgres? Unfortunately, it's not quite as straightforward as the rest. It's not difficult, but it is slightly more involved than what we've seen so far.

Essentially, to "shred" your XML into its different parts, you need to physically parse the XML data using the **XPath**.

If you've used **XPath** before in other places, it's quite straightforward once you get the hang of it, although it can appear confusing at first.

I'm not going to go into too much detail (there are plenty of other guides on **XPath** should you need them), but here's a brief primer.

If we have the following XML snippet:

```
<users>
```

```
    <user>
        <gid>1</gid>
        <name>Peter Shaw</name>
        <email>shawty_ds@yahoo.com</email>
        <webpage>http://shawtyds.wordpress.com</webpage>
    </user>
</users>
```

We can get the value from the name element by using the following path:

```
/users/user/name/text()
```

As you can see, it's rather like navigating your file system. Once you know the path to the file you want (or in this case the element value), you can simply pick it up and use it.

To get our data out using an **XPath**, simply use the **xpath** function (note that where it says "xml abbreviated for readability," you need to copy and paste the XML from the previous XML snippet, or if you're feeling more adventurous, you can also paste the XML from the full user document).

```
select xpath('/users/user/name/text()',xml '…xml abbreviated for readability…')
```

This should return the following result:

Figure 87: xpath

If you pasted just the previous XML, there will be only one entry as shown in the preceding image. If you pasted the full document, there will be as many names as there are user records in the XML you used.

As you can see, the result is an array that contains multiple XML data types. Remember what I was saying previously about **xmlserialize** not having a tag in the string and needing to use **XPath** to ensure you got a string rather than an XML data type? Well here's where you would use it to ensure that happened rather than returning an XML data type.

Another thing to note: If you had multiple occurrences of the result in your path, then the array would have multiple elements in its result array. You'll see how to deal with this in just a moment.

One more thing you need to know before we can write our import routine is how to get your XML file loaded into Postgres.

Postgres has a built-in file loading routine, but it has one big limitation: It cannot access the file system outside of your Postgres data directory.

If you remember from previous chapters, this is the folder within your Postgres installation where Postgres keeps its physical data files. The **Server Configuration** option in the **Tools** menu will remind you if you've forgotten where it is. You can create folders here to organize your files, but you cannot access anything above the root data folder.

There are add-ons for Postgres that allow you to access files outside this folder, and most of the procedural languages such as PL/Perl, PL/PHP, and PL/Python can easily navigate to other files in the file system, but that's beyond the scope of this book.

For now we'll use the **users.xml** that I asked you to save previously (when we exported the users table). Copy this file into a file in the data directory called **users.xml**. (Remember, I'm working on a Windows system.)

Once we do this, we can easily load the file by calling the **pg_read_file()** function like so:

```
select xmlparse(CONTENT pg_read_file('users.xml'))
```

You'll notice we wrap that in a call to **xmlparse** so that we get a proper XML data type to work with.

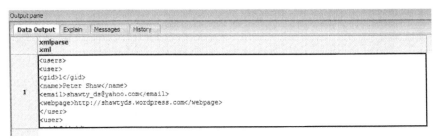

Figure 88: xmlparse

So now that we have all the pieces, what do we do with them? First, we need a Common Table Expression (CTE). A CTE is essentially a temporary table in memory that lasts only for the duration of the query being run.

We use a CTE in this case since we only want to read the file once. If we didn't use a CTE, then we would be rereading the file in every **XPath** function call. While that's not a big deal for our small file here, imagine what it might be like if you were reading a multi-node XML with hundreds of entries.

Once we have a CTE, we chain a second CTE onto our query to actually extract the data using **XPath** into an ordered set, ready to insert into the database.

For those who are not used to using CTEs, they look a little scary at first, but everything is quite simple. The order always flows from top to bottom; if you create a table in the first CTE, it's available in the second and third. If you create a table in the third CTE, it's available only in the output or any CTEs that follow from there. Anything that goes in or is generated above is always available below, a bit like a waterfall.

We could in theory do away with the second CTE and just insert straight from there, but by doing that we would either have to put up with all our data being of an XML data type, or only being able to cast to textual outputs such as **varchar** and **text**.

By using the second CTE, we give ourselves another opportunity to select over the final data set and perform any final data conversions we need. This is important if you have any data that's an integer or number, such as our **gid** column.

xmlserialize and **::<datatype>** from an XML data field can only be cast to a textual output type. You cannot extract a value that's a numerical type and convert it in one step; this is one case where you must use the **cast()** function.

Finally, once we've defined that second CTE, we select over that final set of data, and then use a **select into** statement to create a new table in our database from the converted data. The final query to import our XML data back into Postgres looks like this:

```
with xmldata as

(

        select xmlparse(CONTENT pg_read_file('users.xml'))

),

tabledata as

(

        select

                unnest(xpath('/users/user/gid/text()',(select * from xmldata))) as gid,

                unnest(xpath('/users/user/name/text()',(select * from xmldata))) as
name,

                unnest(xpath('/users/user/email/text()',(select * from xmldata))) as
```

```
email,
            unnest(xpath('/users/user/webpage/text()',(select * from xmldata))) as
webpage
)
select
      cast(xmlserialize(CONTENT gid as text) as integer) as gid,
      name::character varying(50) as name,
      email::character varying(50) as email,
      webpage::character varying(100) as webpage
into
      mytable2
from
      tabledata
```

Not as complicated as it seems from the description, but certainly more involved than some of
what we've seen so far.

Returning Updates

Most developers are familiar with the standard SQL operations **select**, **insert**, **delete**, **update**,
etc.

One thing that's difficult to do, however, is to know exactly what data was affected, and how it
was affected, when performing queries that modify table rows.

We know **select** will always return rows of data, but in other operations we're used to just
seeing something like "1 row(s) affected."

Postgres has a neat trick related to this scenario called a return, as the following example
shows. We'll be using the table we created from our XML in the last section.

```
select * from mytable2
```

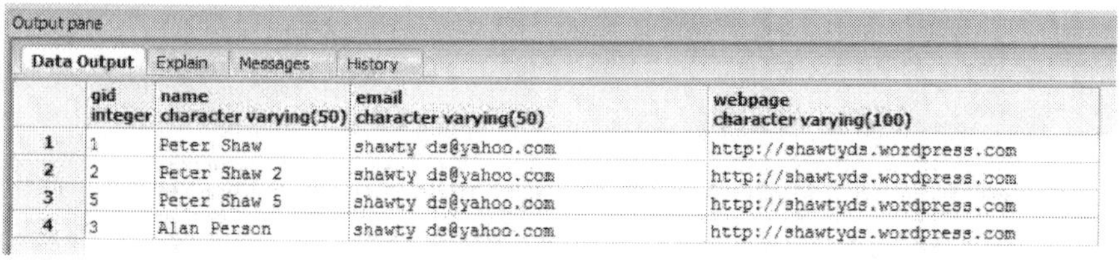
Output pane

Data Output | Explain | Messages | History

	gid integer	name character varying(50)	email character varying(50)	webpage character varying(100)
1	1	Peter Shaw	shawty ds@yahoo.com	http://shawtyds.wordpress.com
2	2	Peter Shaw 2	shawty ds@yahoo.com	http://shawtyds.wordpress.com
3	5	Peter Shaw 5	shawty ds@yahoo.com	http://shawtyds.wordpress.com
4	3	Alan Person	shawty ds@yahoo.com	http://shawtyds.wordpress.com

Figure 89: Output pane

```
delete from mytable2 where gid = 3
```

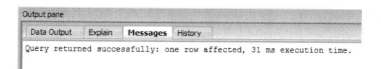

Figure 90: Output pane

And using the **return** statement:

```
select * from mytable2
```

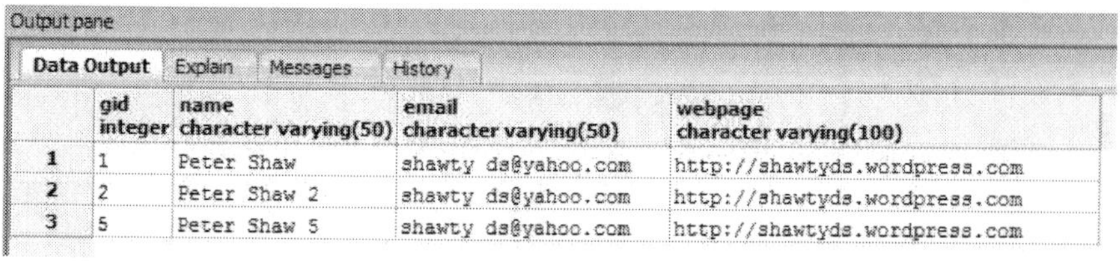
Output pane

Data Output | Explain | Messages | History

	gid integer	name character varying(50)	email character varying(50)	webpage character varying(100)
1	1	Peter Shaw	shawty ds@yahoo.com	http://shawtyds.wordpress.com
2	2	Peter Shaw 2	shawty ds@yahoo.com	http://shawtyds.wordpress.com
3	5	Peter Shaw 5	shawty ds@yahoo.com	http://shawtyds.wordpress.com

Figure 91: Output pane

```
delete from mytable2 where gid = 5 returning *
```

	gid integer	name character varying(50)	email character varying(50)	webpage character varying(100)
1	5	Peter Shaw 5	shawty_ds@yahoo.com	http://shawtyds.wordpress.com

Figure 92: Output pane

```
select * from mytable2
```

	gid integer	name character varying(50)	email character varying(50)	webpage character varying(100)
1	1	Peter Shaw	shawty_ds@yahoo.com	http://shawtyds.wordpress.com
2	2	Peter Shaw 2	shawty_ds@yahoo.com	http://shawtyds.wordpress.com

Figure 93: Output pane

As you can see just by adding **returns** * to the end of our delete statement, the row that was deleted was returned as the result of our query.

Imagine now that if you wanted to create a backup table of all records deleted from the database, you could easily get this data back from your query just as you would with a regular **select** statement, and then you could write it directly into another table quite easily.

This also works with updates.

```
update mytable2 set email = 'me@here.there' where gid = 2 returning *
```

	gid integer	name character varying(50)	email character varying(50)	webpage character varying(100)
1	2	Peter Shaw 2	me@here.there	http://shawtyds.wordpress.com

Figure 94: Output pane

If you do this with an update you get a copy of the updated row sent back to you. Usually to get the updated data you would normally have to perform the update, and then follow that with a regular **select** to select the new data.

Inserts do exactly the same thing.

```
insert into mytable2 values(6,'a second
person','anemail@somwhere.com','http://aweb.page.com/') returning *
```

Output pane

Data Output	Explain	Messages	History	
	gid integer	name character varying(50)	email character varying(50)	webpage character varying(100)
1	6	a second person	anemail@somwhere.com	http://aweb.page.com/

Figure 95: Output pane

You'll notice that in each of the previous examples I'm using **returning** *. As with any SQL query, when you use *, it means return everything.

If you only want the **gid** column, then you can use a regular column identifier as you would in a normal **select** statement:

```
insert into mytable2 values(7,'a third
person','anemail@somwhere.com','http://aweb.page.com/') returning gid
```

Figure 96: Output pane

I'll leave you to explore other possibilities here, but because it's a regular SQL construct you can use functions, aggregations, and most other Postgres features to use the returned data in some very clever ways, one of which we are going to explore next.

Writeable CTEs

I've already introduced you to CTEs in the section on XML; however, it's not something that's commonly known or used in many databases.

Microsoft SQL Server has had CTEs available for some time, and I have used them to solve many real-world problems where I needed to work with temporary tables, but I've not yet seen them used on a regular basis by other developers.

Classically however, CTEs have always been read-only, that is, you've only ever been able to do select-based queries using them.

Starting from Postgres v9.1 you can now perform inserts, updates, and deletes on a CTE. This opens up some very interesting possibilities.

Let's start with a real-world example. Using the test database you created, let's add some new tables. I'm just going to give you the SQL here, but feel free to use **pgAdmin** to create them using the GUI.

```
create table items_in_stock
(
        storename text,

        itemname text,

        amountavailable int not null,

        costperitem numeric(16,2) not null
);
insert into items_in_stock values
('store 1','orangething', 45, 20.00),

('store 1','bluething', 50, 25.00),

('store 1','purplething', 30, 30.00),

('store 2','orangething', 60, 20.00),

('store 2','bluething', 10, 25.00),

('store 2','purplething', 25, 30.00);


create table sales_made
(
        recordid serial primary key,

        storename text,

        itemname text,

        amountsold int not null
```

```
);

insert into sales_made(storename, itemname, amountsold) values

('store 1', 'orangething', 5),

('store 2', 'bluething', 1),

('store 2', 'purplething', 10),

('store 1', 'bluething', 15),

('store 2', 'orangething', 10),

('store 1', 'bluething', 15);
```

Now let's suppose we'd like to see a report of the before and after stock amounts, and how much had been made in each store based on the sales made.

First, let's start with a normal read-only CTE that can summarize things easily:

```
with all_sales as

(

        select

                storename as storename,

                itemname as itemname,

                sum(amountsold) as totalamountsold

        from

                sales_made group by storename,itemname

),

sales_report as

(

        select

                iis.storename as storename,

                iis.itemname as itemname,

                iis.amountavailable as originalamountavailable,
```

```
        als.totalamountsold as amountsold,

        iis.amountavailable - als.totalamountsold as newamountavailable,

        iis.costperitem as costperitem,

        iis.costperitem * als.totalamountsold as amountmadeinsales


    from items_in_stock as iis

        join all_sales als on als.storename = iis.storename AND als.itemname =
iis.itemname

)

select * from sales_report
```

This code should result in the following:

	storename text	itemname text	originalamountavailable integer	amountsold bigint	newamountavailable bigint	costperitem numeric(16,2)	amountmadeinsales numeric
1	store 1	orangething	45	5	40	20.00	100.00
2	store 1	bluething	50	30	20	25.00	750.00
3	store 2	orangething	60	10	50	20.00	200.00
4	store 2	bluething	10	1	9	25.00	25.00
5	store 2	purplething	25	10	15	30.00	300.00

Figure 97: Output pane

As you can see, we are shown only those items that have been sold, how many we previously had, and how many we have now. We can also see how much we made from those sales.

Now the only problem we have is that the data we see is only in memory—our tables have not been updated in any way. Now we need to push those changes into our items in stock table.

We can do that easily by rewriting our query as follows:

```
with all_sales as

(

    select

            storename as storename,

            itemname as itemname,
```

```
                sum(amountsold) as totalamountsold

        from

                sales_made group by storename,itemname
),

sales_report as

(

        select

                iis.storename as storename,

                iis.itemname as itemname,

                iis.amountavailable as originalamountavailable,

                als.totalamountsold as amountsold,

                iis.amountavailable - als.totalamountsold as newamountavailable,

                iis.costperitem as costperitem,

                iis.costperitem * als.totalamountsold as amountmadeinsales


        from items_in_stock as iis

        join all_sales als on als.storename = iis.storename AND als.itemname =
iis.itemname
),

items_update as

(

        update items_in_stock iis

                set amountavailable = sr.newamountavailable

        from

                sales_report sr

        where

                sr.storename = iis.storename AND sr.itemname = iis.itemname
```

```
returning

        iis.storename as storename,

        iis.itemname as itemname,

        sr.originalamountavailable as originalamountavailable,

        sr.amountsold as amountsold,

        iis.amountavailable as newamountavailable,

        iis.costperitem as costperitem,

        sr.amountmadeinsales as amountmadeinsales

)

select * from items_update
```

Output pane

	storename text	itemname text	originalamountavailable integer	amountsold bigint	newamountavailable integer	costperitem numeric(16,2)	amountmadeinsales numeric
1	store 1	orangething	45	5	40	20.00	100.00
2	store 1	bluething	50	30	20	25.00	750.00
3	store 2	orangething	60	10	50	20.00	200.00
4	store 2	bluething	10	1	9	25.00	25.00
5	store 2	purplething	25	10	15	30.00	300.00

Figure 98: Output pane

We get the same output as we did previously, only this time you'll notice we've added a third CTE to the chain.

This CTE has in it an **update** statement that actually updates the underlying **items_in_stock** table with the new values calculated in the **sales_report** CTE.

The result is that not only do we get our sales report returned, but our original data also gets updated for us in the process, all in a single SQL statement.

There is no need for creating separate temporary tables, or selecting data in those temporary tables to perform the updates separately. You didn't even need to put this into a stored procedure or database function either. Sometimes Postgres just makes solving the problem at hand a breeze.

Special Data Types

Our final section on Postgres-specific SQL will cover some of the unique data types that are available in the database.

You've already been introduced to the XML data type; now it's time to meet some of the others that can only be found in Postgres. Note that I'm only going to cover data types that are built into the system. Postgres, like many database systems, can be extended in many ways, including having new data types added to it. What I aim to show in this last section doesn't require any such add-ons.

Geometry

Even without an extension such as PostGIS, Postgres has some basic geometry types by default, such as:

- point
- line
- lseg
- box
- path
- polygon
- circle

For the purposes of this book I'll just show the simple ones. You can read details about the rest in the Postgres manual at http://www.postgresql.org/docs/9.2/static/datatype-geometric.html.

Let's create a table of points:

```
create table geometry(

    recordid serial primary key,

    thedot point

)
```

Now let's add some data:

```
insert into geometry(thedot) values

    (point'(1,1)'),

    (point'(2,2)'),

    (point'(3,3)'),

    (point'(4,4)')
```

As you can see, you need to specify the data type you're adding. Unlike other data types, you can't use :: to cast a type at insert time, and specifying it on its own in parentheses is reserved for things like records and arrays.

```
select * from geometry
```

This line gives us:

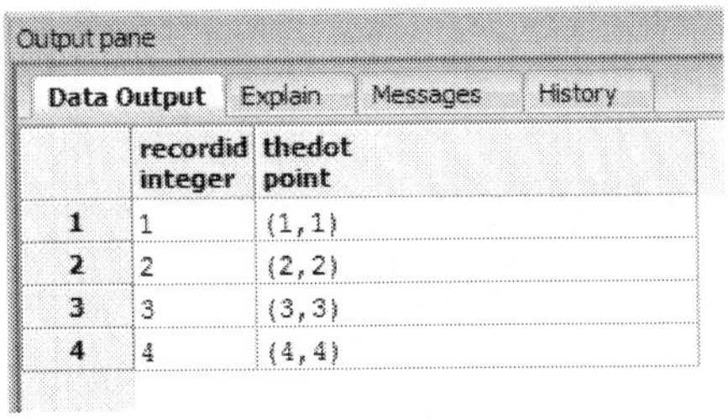

	recordid integer	thedot point
1	1	(1,1)
2	2	(2,2)
3	3	(3,3)
4	4	(4,4)

Figure 99: Table of points

Now let's create some circles and lines.

```
create table geometry2(

    recordid serial primary key,

    theline lseg

)
create table geometry3(

    recordid serial primary key,

    thecircle circle

)
```

And we'll insert some data:

```
insert into geometry2(theline) values

    (lseg '((1,1),(2,2))'),
```

```
    (lseg '((3,3),(4,4))')

insert into geometry3(thecircle) values

    (circle '((1,1),1)'),

    (circle '((3,3),1)')
```

Line segments are created by specifying a start x position and y position, and an end x position and y position. Circles are created by specifying a center x position and y position, and a radius.

In our previous example we created a table with two lines from 1,1 to 2,2, and 3,3 to 4,4. We then created two circles, each with a radius of 1 unit at positions 1,1 and 3,3 respectively.

Once you have your data in your various tables, it should come as no surprise that there are a number of powerful functions that allow you to do all sorts of operations on the geometry you have stored. For example, to translate all your points by (1,1):

```
select * from geometry
```

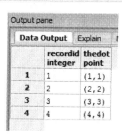

Figure 100: Points to translate

```
select

    recordid,

    thedot + point '(1,1)' as thedot

from geometry
```

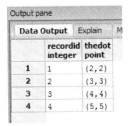

Figure 101: Translated points

Or to calculate the distance between our two circles:

```
select

    (select thecircle from geometry3 where recordid = 1)

    <->

    (select thecircle from geometry3 where recordid = 2)

    as distance
```

Figure 102: Calculated distance

There are many more functions and operators. A full list can be found at
http://www.postgresql.org/docs/9.2/static/functions-geometry.html.

Network address types

Postgres also has a built-in data type for handling network address data such as IP addresses
and MAC addresses. These addresses are the numbers used to connect computers and other
devices to networks like the Internet.

An IP address you may have seen before is 127.0.0.1.

This is otherwise known as a **localhost** (I mentioned this previously in the section on
installation), a software-level address allocated by the network software on the device.

Further down the chain is the unique hardware address that all devices have, called the MAC address. It usually looks something like this 00:16:E6:8E:BE:85.

Postgres can natively handle these data types. More importantly, when selecting, grouping, and sorting, it is aware of how to order them correctly.

As well as being able to store and manipulate them, you can also specify a network mask by using the forward slash notation: 192.168.100.0/24.

This would specify a network residing in 192.168.100 with a network mask of 24 bits, which means a class C network residing at network number 192.168.100 with hosts ranging from 0 to 255.

Unlike many of the other data types, there are no special functions for handling these data types. The strength in using them comes from the ability to search, index, and sort them natively at high speeds, while many other database systems have to handle them using strings and full text searches, which is very often inefficient.

The manual page for the network types can be found at http://www.postgresql.org/docs/9.2/static/datatype-net-types.html.

More data types?

Absolutely.

We have the ones you might expect, such as **Numeric**, **Monetary**, **Date/Time**, and **Binary**.

Then we have things like **Json**, **UUID** (Universal IDs similar to .NET GUIDs), **Bit Strings**, **Number Ranges**, **Composite Record Types**, **Object Identifiers**, and more. A full list can be found at http://www.postgresql.org/docs/9.2/static/datatype.html.

Chapter 8 PostGIS

No book on Postgres would be complete without at least mentioning PostGIS, one of the biggest reasons for the success of Postgres. This one simple addition has put Postgres at the forefront of most of the world's open source (and many closed source) mapping and geographical information systems.

In fact, next to Postgres and PostGIS, the next most used database technology is Oracle Spatial, which costs much more and is generally out of reach of most small to medium-sized enterprises.

I can't possibly cover everything that PostGIS is capable of in this chapter, so it's going to be fairly brief. For a more in-depth look at GIS (and PostGIS), see my previous book in the *Succinctly* series, *GIS Succinctly*, which covers GIS as its main topic.

So what does PostGIS bring to the table?

First of all, PostGIS adds many new data types. Some are an extension of the geometric types we've already seen, and others are completely new.

It also adds many (hundreds) of processing functions covering everything from handling vector-based graphics and input shapes, to coordinate conversion based on different grid systems in use around the world.

The most recent versions of PostGIS have been extended to provide many new raster analysis functions and are now so powerful that many of them can take raw bitmap imagery of a scanned paper map or aerial photo and actually extract vector details into a database table from it.

Let's create a new database that's set up to use PostGIS, and then take a quick look at what is added. Open pgAdmin, and follow the instructions in previous chapters for creating a database.

When it comes to selecting the template, make sure you select the template that the PostGIS install added for you.

Figure 103: New Database Properties

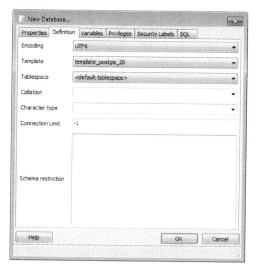

Figure 104: New Database Definition

This template should be called **template_postgis_20** if you followed the previous installation instructions.

Click **OK** and let Postgres create your new database.

Once your database is created, expand the object tree and take a look at what's been added.

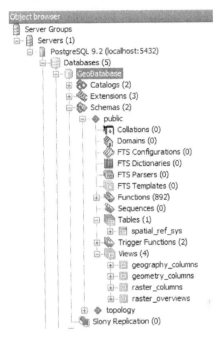

Figure 105: Object tree

One table containing spatial reference information, two trigger functions used to enforce dimensions and geometry types, four views to help manage your GIS database's metadata, and 892 new functions and routines have been added.

If you scroll down through the list of functions you'll see that many of them start with **st_**. These functions are Open Geo Consortium (OGC) compatible functions that follow the simple features standard.

With these functions present, any software that is written to use OSG standards can use Postgres as a GIS store with little or no effort. It also means that a lot of software that works with systems such as Oracle Spatial will have no problems working with Postgres.

You should also see that you have many translation functions such as **ST_Transform()**, which can convert worldwide geometry from one coordinate space to another.

There are many different output functions such as **ST_AsGeoJson()**, **ST_AsKml()**, and **ST_AsGml()**, which allow you to produce GeoJson, Google Earth KML, and industry-standard GML files directly from mapping data stored in your database.

Finally on top of all of this, if you look in the installation folder where you stored Postgres on your hard drive, you should also find a number of extra tools such as shp2pgsql:

Figure 106: Installed Postgres tools

This tool converts industry-standard shapefiles into SQL scripts so they can be inserted into Postgres.

If you look in the **postgisgui** folder, you should also find a graphical version of these tools, which allows you to simply choose GIS data files from your local hard drive and automate the insertion process.

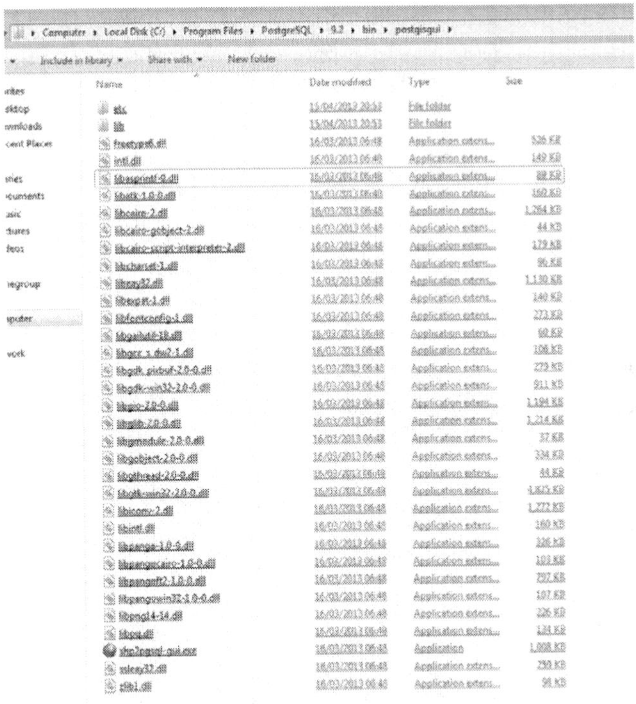

Figure 107: Postgisgui folder

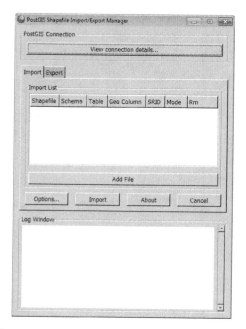

Figure 108: PostGIS Shapefile Import/Export Manager

Getting started using GIS has never been easier. No more reading dozens of books on the subject and attending expensive courses required.

With the liberal Postgres open source license, the PostGIS add-on, plus many of the free geospatial applications that exist these days such as Quantum GIS, there's no reason why a good GIS system is a difficult thing to find.

I encourage you to go further on this topic; it's something that I find exceptionally interesting, and I'm sure you will too.

Chapter 9 Using Postgres with .NET

So now we get to the fun part: using Postgres in a .NET application.

I'm not going to use any of the special functionality that Postgres has available in this example; it's going to be a quick and easy editing application that will edit MyTable that we created previously.

We'll start first with the ADO.NET version. Once that's working, we'll convert it to use Entity Framework version 5.

Both sample applications are available for download at https://bitbucket.org/syncfusion/postgres_succinctly as two separate projects, one for the plain ADO version, and the other for the Entity Framework version.

Note that I'll be using Visual Studio 2010 for my examples here, but feel free to use whatever compiler or IDE you wish. The code I present should work under any C# compiler, including Mono. Npgsql (the .NET data interface for Postgres) is known to work well under Mono, but I can't guarantee that the Entity Framework version will. Remember, I'm using a Windows 7 platform for this example.

Create a simple Windows Forms application

We'll start by firing up Visual Studio 2010, starting a new project from the **File** menu, and selecting a **Windows Forms** project that targets .NET 4.

Figure 109: Windows Forms project

Once you've set your path, project name, etc., click **OK** to create your project in the IDE.

Once your project is created, resize your main window to approximately 650 × 530 pixels, and then add a tab control and two normal buttons to the main form.

Your two buttons should be **Cancel** and **Edit**.

On the first tab control page, place a regular **DataGridView** and a third button marked **Load Data**. Name the first tab **View Data**. When you're finished, your form should look something like this:

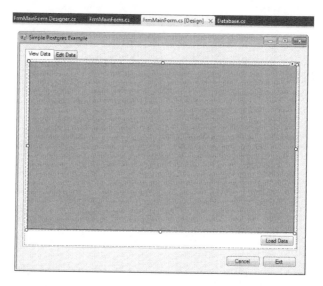

Figure 110: Application window

I've left the data grid at its defaults, (automatic columns, widths, etc.). We'll be populating this in code soon.

Once you've completed first tab, switch to the second and place a **Table Layout Panel** on it. Edit the **layouts** columns and rows to the following:

Column1 15%

Column2 85%

Row1 30 pixels

Row2 30 pixels

Row3 30 pixels

Row4 30 pixels

Row5 Autosize

Next, add a label to every left-hand cell in the table control and set the **Dock** property to **Fill**. Set the **text alignment** of each label to **middle-right** except for the bottom one, which should be **top-right**, and then give each label the following text:

Gid :

Name :

EMail :

Webpage :

Biography :

Continue by adding another label in the top right cell of the table layout (same row as **Gid**) and text boxes in the remaining cells.

The bottom cell's text box should be set to **Multiline**. Set the **Dock** property on all of them to **Fill**.

Once you've finished the table layout, add six buttons across the bottom of the tab page and label them from left to right as follows:

<<

Create New

Insert

Update

Delete

>>

Once you're finished, your form should look something like the following:

Figure 111: Completed form

Once the interface is complete, we need to start adding code. First though, we need to add the **NpgSql** assembly using **NuGet**.

Right-click **References**, and then select **Manage NuGet Packages**. Ensure you're searching online. Then in **Search**, type **Npgsql**. You should see the following:

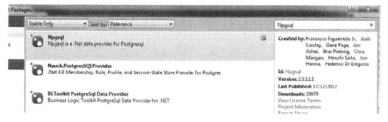

Figure 112: Adding the Npgsql assembly

Click the **Install** button next to **Npgsql** to install it in your project.

Next, right-click on your project root and add two new folders, one called **classes** and one called **entities**. Note: You don't have to organize your project this way, but I always do as it makes for easier management. If you're at all curious about my approach, I have a 90-minute video about the subject available free on the LIDNUG YouTube page at http://www.youtube.com/user/lidnug.

In the **Classes** folder, create two new classes called **ConnectionStrings.cs** and **Database.cs**. In the **Entities** folder, create a class called **MyTable.cs**.

ConnectionStrings.cs is required to get the connection string from the **app.config** file as **Npgsql** does not have the ability to take a connection string name and load the real string from it. We use the **ConnectionStrings** class to get the string, and then pass that to the methods in **DataBase.cs** where all the functionality to talk to Postgres is.

The entity class should model your database table.

In our case the three classes appear as follows:

ConnectionStrings.cs

```
using System;
using System.Configuration;

namespace PostgresExample.Classes
{
  public static class ConnectionStrings
  {
    public static string PgConnection
    {
      get
      {
        const string connectionStringName = "pgconnection";
        if
(string.IsNullOrEmpty(ConfigurationManager.ConnectionStrings[connectionStringName].Connec
tionString))
        {
          throw new Exception("Connection string (" + connectionStringName + ") not
defined in app.config!");
        }

        return
ConfigurationManager.ConnectionStrings[connectionStringName].ConnectionString;
      }
    }

  }
}
```

Database.cs

```
using System.Collections.Generic;
using Npgsql;
using NpgsqlTypes;
using PostgresExample.Entities;

namespace PostgresExample.Classes
{
  public class Database
  {
```

```csharp
public List<MyTable> GetAll()
{
    List<MyTable> results = new List<MyTable>();

    using (NpgsqlConnection connection = new
NpgsqlConnection(ConnectionStrings.PgConnection))
    {
        connection.Open();
        const string sql = "select * from mytable";
        using (NpgsqlCommand command = new NpgsqlCommand(sql, connection))
        {
            using (NpgsqlDataReader reader = command.ExecuteReader())
            {
                if (!reader.HasRows) return results;
                while (reader.Read())
                {
                    results.Add(new MyTable
                        {
                            Gid = (int)reader["gid"],
                            Name = (string)reader["name"],
                            Email = (string)reader["email"],
                            Webpage = (string)reader["webpage"],
                            Bio = (string)reader["bio"]
                        });
                }
            }
        }
    }

    return results;
}

public MyTable GetByGid(int gid)
{
    MyTable result;

    using (NpgsqlConnection connection = new
NpgsqlConnection(ConnectionStrings.PgConnection))
    {
        connection.Open();
        const string sql = "select * from mytable where gid = :gid";
        using (NpgsqlCommand command = new NpgsqlCommand(sql, connection))
        {
            command.Parameters.Add(new NpgsqlParameter("gid", NpgsqlDbType.Integer));
            command.Parameters["gid"].Value = gid;

            using (NpgsqlDataReader reader = command.ExecuteReader())
            {
                if (!reader.HasRows) return null;
                reader.Read();
                result = new MyTable
                {
                    Gid = (int)reader["gid"],
                    Name = (string)reader["name"],
                    Email = (string)reader["email"],
                    Webpage = (string)reader["webpage"],
                    Bio = (string)reader["bio"]
                };
```

```csharp
            }
          }
      }

      return result;
  }

  public void AddNew(MyTable entity)
  {
      using (NpgsqlConnection connection = new
NpgsqlConnection(ConnectionStrings.PgConnection))
      {
          connection.Open();
          const string sql = "insert into mytable(name, email, webpage, bio)
values(:name,:email,:webpage,:bio)";
          using(NpgsqlCommand command = new NpgsqlCommand(sql, connection))
          {
            command.Parameters.Add(new NpgsqlParameter("name", NpgsqlDbType.Varchar));
            command.Parameters.Add(new NpgsqlParameter("email", NpgsqlDbType.Varchar));
            command.Parameters.Add(new NpgsqlParameter("webpage", NpgsqlDbType.Varchar));
            command.Parameters.Add(new NpgsqlParameter("bio", NpgsqlDbType.Varchar));
            command.Parameters["name"].Value = entity.Name;
            command.Parameters["email"].Value = entity.Email;
            command.Parameters["webpage"].Value = entity.Webpage;
            command.Parameters["bio"].Value = entity.Bio;

            command.ExecuteNonQuery();
          }
      }
  }

  public void DeleteByGid(int gid)
  {
      using (NpgsqlConnection connection = new
NpgsqlConnection(ConnectionStrings.PgConnection))
      {
          connection.Open();
          const string sql = "delete from mytable where gid = :gid";
          using (NpgsqlCommand command = new NpgsqlCommand(sql, connection))
          {
            command.Parameters.Add(new NpgsqlParameter("gid", NpgsqlDbType.Integer));
            command.Parameters["gid"].Value = gid;

            command.ExecuteNonQuery();
          }
      }
  }

  public void Update(MyTable entity)
  {
      using (NpgsqlConnection connection = new
NpgsqlConnection(ConnectionStrings.PgConnection))
      {
          connection.Open();
          const string sql = "update mytable set name = :name, email = :email, webpage =
:webpage, bio = :bio WHERE gid = :gid";
          using (NpgsqlCommand command = new NpgsqlCommand(sql, connection))
          {
```

```
            command.Parameters.Add(new NpgsqlParameter("name", NpgsqlDbType.Varchar));
            command.Parameters.Add(new NpgsqlParameter("email", NpgsqlDbType.Varchar));
            command.Parameters.Add(new NpgsqlParameter("webpage", NpgsqlDbType.Varchar));
            command.Parameters.Add(new NpgsqlParameter("bio", NpgsqlDbType.Varchar));
            command.Parameters.Add(new NpgsqlParameter("gid", NpgsqlDbType.Integer));
            command.Parameters["name"].Value = entity.Name;
            command.Parameters["email"].Value = entity.Email;
            command.Parameters["webpage"].Value = entity.Webpage;
            command.Parameters["bio"].Value = entity.Bio;
            command.Parameters["gid"].Value = entity.Gid;

            command.ExecuteNonQuery();
        }
      }

    }
  }
}
```

MyTable.cs

```
namespace PostgresExample.Entities
{
  public class MyTable
  {
    public int Gid { get; set; }
    public string Name { get; set; }
    public string Email { get; set; }
    public string Webpage { get; set; }
    public string Bio { get; set; }

  }
}
```

As you can see, the code is straightforward and relatively easy to understand.

If you get any missing reference errors when trying to compile, you'll need to use **Add Reference Tools** in Visual Studio to add a reference to **System.Configuration**. This is required to read the configuration string in **ConnectionStrings.cs**.

The key to opening a connection to Postgres lies with the **using** statement, which ensures the object is disposed of correctly.

```
using (NpgsqlConnection connection = new
NpgsqlConnection(ConnectionStrings.PgConnection))
{
      connection.Open();
}
```

Once you have the connection, you can create an **Npgsql** command object to allow you to execute standard SQL statements.

```
const string sql = "select * from mytable";
using (NpgsqlCommand command = new NpgsqlCommand(sql, connection))
{
}
```

Again, we employ the **using** statement (since the object derives from **IDisposable**) to ensure that the object is disposed of correctly.

If you need to pass parameters into your SQL string, then you should use the parameterized functionality that exists in ADO.NET to protect against things like XSS and SQL injection attacks.

You can also use **string.format** or some other form of concatenation, but it is highly unadvisable to do so unless you're completely sure your input data is clean.

```
command.Parameters.Add(new NpgsqlParameter("gid", NpgsqlDbType.Integer));
command.Parameters["gid"].Value = entity.Gid;
```

Where you specify the parameter name in the previous code sample, you would place : followed by the name in your SQL string (in this case :**gid**).

After all of that is set up, it's simply a case of calling the following if your SQL is not expected to return any data:

```
command.ExecuteNonQuery();
```

If your SQL is expected to return data, then call:

```
command.ExecuteReader();
```

The rest, such as working with data readers, is all standard ADO.NET code.

Once you have those three classes in place, you need to add the connection string to the **app.config** file in the application. The connection string should look something like the following:

```
<?xml version="1.0"?>
<configuration>

  <startup>
    <supportedRuntime version="v4.0" sku=".NETFramework,Version=v4.0"/>
  </startup>

  <connectionStrings>
    <add name="pgconnection"
         connectionString="Server=virtw7-lucinda;Port=5432;Database=mydatabase;User
Id=myuser;Password=myuser;"
```

```
                providerName="Npgsql" />
    </connectionStrings>

</configuration>
```

If you're running this application on the same machine you installed Postgres, then the previous code sample will work as is. If not, you'll need to change the parameters as required to point to the correct server.

Once we get to this point, all that remains to be done is to wire up the UI buttons and elements to the various methods in the **Database** class.

Please refer to the download for the full code. I'm not going to paste the full form code here, as it's quite long. I've also added some extra functionality to make the UI more friendly, but these extras are not necessary to demonstrate how to use Postgres.

The key thing here is the **Database** class and the way it acts as a proxy between the classes representing your table data and your program code.

If you're using raw **Npgsql**, then you should definitely take a look at the manual page available at http://npgsql.projects.pgfoundry.org/docs/manual/UserManual.html.

There is so much more that is available, especially in release 2. Things like prepared statements, stored procedure support, and reference cursors are now available, along with bulk table imports and exports, and many other features.

Once you have the app running, on the first tab you should see this:

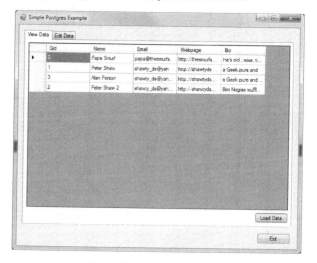

Figure 113: View Data tab

And on the second tab:

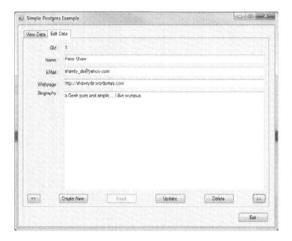

Figure 114: Edit Data tab

Converting the App to Use Entity Framework

For this final part, we'll take our ADO.NET-based app, and only change what we need to make it work with Entity Framework 5 Code First.

You won't need to make any changes to the GUI code since we'll use the existing **DataBase.cs** class to provide the same interface to our app as the ADO.NET version.

For this part you can delete the **ConnectionStrings.cs** class in your **classes** folder, and create a new class called **EFDataBase.cs**.

You also need to use **NuGet** as you did previously, and add **Entity Framework** to your project. (At the time of writing this book, v5 was the current version.)

EFDatabase.cs should contain the following code:

```
using System.Data.Entity;
using PostgresExample.Entities;

namespace PostgresExample.Classes
{
  public class EFDatabase : DbContext
  {
    public EFDatabase()
      : base("pgconnection") // Name of connection string to look for.
    { }
```

```
    public DbSet<MyTable> MyTables { get; set; }

  }
}
```

This is the main interface between our code and Entity Framework. Any of the many tutorials available on the Internet will explain what's going on here.

Once we have the Entity Framework interface ready, we need to adapt our **Database.cs** class so that it looks as follows:

```
using System.Collections.Generic;
using System.Data;
using System.Data.Entity.Infrastructure;
using System.Linq;
using PostgresExample.Entities;

namespace PostgresExample.Classes
{
  public class Database
  {
    public List<MyTable> GetAll()
    {
      List<MyTable> results;

      using(EFDatabase myDb = new EFDatabase())
      {
        results = myDb.Set<MyTable>().AsQueryable().ToList();
      }

      return results;
    }

    public void AddNew(MyTable entity)
    {
      using (EFDatabase myDb = new EFDatabase())
      {
        myDb.Set<MyTable>().Add(entity);
        myDb.SaveChanges();
      }

    }

    public void DeleteByGid(int gid)
    {
      using(EFDatabase myDb = new EFDatabase())
      {
        MyTable entityToRemove = myDb.Set<MyTable>().FirstOrDefault(x => x.Gid == gid);
        if (entityToRemove == null) return;
        myDb.Set<MyTable>().Remove(entityToRemove);
        myDb.SaveChanges();
      }

    }

    public void Update(MyTable entity)
```

```
{
  using(EFDatabase myDb = new EFDatabase())
  {

    DbEntityEntry entry = myDb.Entry(entity);
    if (entry != null)
    {
      switch (entry.State)
      {
        case EntityState.Detached:
          myDb.Set<MyTable>().Attach(entity);
          myDb.Entry(entity).State = EntityState.Modified;
          break;

        case EntityState.Deleted:
          entry.CurrentValues.SetValues(entity);
          entry.State = EntityState.Modified;
          break;

        default:
          entry.State = EntityState.Modified;
          break;
      }
    }
    else
    {
      myDb.Set<MyTable>().Attach(entity);
      myDb.Entry(entity).State = EntityState.Modified;
    }

    myDb.ChangeTracker.DetectChanges();
    myDb.SaveChanges();

  }

}
}
```

There is much less code than in the ADO.NET database class, but this does come at a price. Entity Framework is much slower than plain ADO.NET. It's worth noting that many of the micro ORMs such as **Simple.Data**, **Massive**, and **ServiceStack** all support Postgres. I can highly recommend **Simple.Data**, as I've used it for many projects where Postgres has been the main store.

Once the data classes are set, you need to make some changes to your **MyTable** entity class.

These changes involve adding Entity Framework data attributes to the class to set the default schema (which is always **public** under Postgres) and making sure the column names are lowercase.

Note also that when using **CodeFirst** in Entity Framework with **NpgSql**, you must create your tables by hand. Entity Framework with Postgres will not currently create non-existing tables for you.

After you make the changes to your entity, it should look something like the following:

```csharp
using System.ComponentModel.DataAnnotations;
using System.ComponentModel.DataAnnotations.Schema;

namespace PostgresExample.Entities
{
    // Note: I'm using column attributes to enforce lowercase names and set the default
    schema which is 'public'

    [Table("mytable", Schema = "public")]
    public class MyTable
    {
        [Key]
        [Column("gid")]
        public int Gid { get; set; }

        [Column("name")]
        public string Name { get; set; }

        [Column("email")]
        public string Email { get; set; }

        [Column("webpage")]
        public string Webpage { get; set; }

        [Column("bio")]
        public string Bio { get; set; }

    }
}
```

Once the code changes are finished, the last thing to do is to register **Npgsql** in your app config as a data provider by using the following addition:

```xml
<system.data>
    <DbProviderFactories>
        <add name="Npgsql Data Provider"
            invariant="Npgsql"
            description="Data Provider for PostgreSQL"
            type="Npgsql.NpgsqlFactory, Npgsql" />
    </DbProviderFactories>
</system.data>
```

Without this section in your application config file, you'll get an exception when you try to connect stating that the registered data provider was not found.

If everything has worked as planned, then pressing **F5** and running your app should give you the same output as the previous ADO.NET example.

Made in the USA
San Bernardino, CA
01 September 2018